Kick-ass Testimonials

A captivating account of how one of the giants of jazz in the 20th century was also a giant in the kitchen. It's fun to imagine Mr. Blakey shopping for ingredients at the Reading Terminal Market, before my time.

Paul Steinke, General Manager, Reading Terminal Market, Philadelphia, PA

I am happy she wrote about Art. We need more about his legacy spread everywhere.

Donald Harrison, Jr., New Orleans saxophonist and Jazz Messengers alumnus

I believe if you start with great food, you don't have to do much with it. The food will speak for itself. Art Blakey's fresh seafood, fruits, and vegetables are speaking up loud and clear.

Chef Thomas Ramsey of Foundation Room, House of Blues, Atlantic City

Art all gussied up and makin' it happen.

ART BLAKEY COOKIN' AND JAMMIN'
Recipes and Remembrances from a Jazz Life

by

Sandy Warren

Foreword by Mac Rebennack

(Dr. John)

Margaret Media, Inc

2010

Published by Margaret Media, Inc.

Cover and book design by Molly Ebert

Printed in the U.S.A. by
Sheridan Books, Chelsea, Michigan

ISBN 978-0-984551-2-8
Library of Congress Control Number 2010932840

618 Mississippi Street
Donaldsonville, LA 70346
(225) 473-9319
www.margaretmedia.com

Cover photo by Hal Wilson
Courtesy of EMI Records Limited and Capitol Records, LLC

Fifteen percent of net profits will be contributed to the New Orleans Musicians' Clinic. Thank you, Mac, for tuning me in to this sacred space where minds, bodies and spirits are nurtured and healed.

In peace and love,

Sandy

Addendum: A portion of the profits will go also to Voice of the Wetlands in loving memory of Bobby Charles who died before this book was finished.

Our three basic needs – for food and security and love – are so mixed and mingled and entwined that we cannot straightly think of one without the others.

MFK Fisher, Food Writer

From the beginning of human existence on earth, people of all cultures have found solace and communion in both food and storytelling.

Colleen Sell, Food Writer

Food is our common ground, a universal experience.

James Beard, Chef and Food Writer

To musicians, music lovers, and foodies blessed
with a New Orleans heart and soul no matter
where you are on the planets. Especially to you, Mac, with
never ending love and admiration.

Photos courtesy of Sandy Warren

Takashi boppin' around town with Atsuko and Art.

Acknowledgements

A book, like a life, is not created apart from others.   Sheila Bender

Thankfulness to:

Bob Scherer, my longtime friend, for supporting me in this sometimes emotionally draining endeavor from the time it was just a jumble of ideas and memories in my head until it became a printed recollection to be shared with others.

Tim Greene - son, soul mate, best friend - for your unwavering belief in me and all that I do, your listening ear, and for being the constant in my work, my life.

Nick Regine - passionate writing coach/consultant, friend, and counselor - for providing the structure and continuity without which this book still wouldn't be finished.

Mac Rebennack (Dr. John), my main muse, for burrowing way down deep into my heart and soul and being my 24/7 sweet inspiration. If I were to acknowledge all the ways you have enriched my life and this book, it would fill another book.

Jay Bourgoyne, author, friend, and proprietor of my favorite guest house on Bourbon Street for the foresight to know the absolutely right publisher for me would be Mary Gehman.

Mary Gehman, thank you for agreeing with Jay.

Eternal gratefulness also goes to:

Allison Moonitz for typing what I had scribbled.

Elaine Christopher, Dominic Fulginiti, and Joan Roof for feeding me goodies fit for the gods when I was too busy writing about food to cook any.

Sue and Al Jacobson for providing me a sweet home in New Orleans when I needed to be there to take care of business.

Shannon Powell, New Orleans drummer extraordinaire, who believed in this book from the moment you heard about it and spread the word wherever you went.

Jay Tyburski, talented photographer and jack of all trades, for encouraging words and snapping those pics of me at the French Market.

Each one of you at WWOZ Radio New Orleans for stirrin' my soul with the music and conversation and being my muse 'round midnight and every other hour.

Frank Barnard, Kenny Olin, and Josh Eaton at the UPS Store in the Taj for all the copying, scanning, and mailing, and smiling that enabled this book to come together.

Takashi Blakey, dear son, for filling in the blanks and reaching out to Bruce Lundvall.

Bruce Lundvall, president of Blue Note Records, for opening the way for me to get permission to use the only picture I ever envisioned for the book cover.

Ray Osnato, Don Sickler, Lee Mergner, Michael Cuscuna, Tab Benoit, and John Ramsay for your consultations.

Martin Kaelin, photographer, for being my Philadelphia go-to-guy.

Bethany Bultman, friend and supporter, for being my livin', walkin', talkin' file on New Orleans resources.

Deb Collins for being my webmaster and so much more.

Wallace Boudreaux for your unwavering support.

All the photographers and artists whose works brought this book to life and Cynthia Sesso for your invaluable efforts in getting me the rights to use priceless photos taken long ago in Europe.

Daniel Hammer at the Historic New Orleans Collection for coming up with a pic of Art from the 1972 Jazz Fest.

Marie Schleinkofer, best friend, for always being there to do whatever whenever.

The Lower 911 Band - Herman Ernest III, drums; David Barard, bass; and John Fohl, guitar - for all the inspiration and good vibes in the live concerts and backstage chats.

James Lemkin, Sherry Beth Mounce, and Stephanie O'Quin for your positivity.

Donald Harrison, Thomas Ramsey, Paul Steinke, Jelly Roll Justice, and Bobby Watson for believing in me and the book and writing those kick-ass testimonials.

Photo by Phil Turner

Dr. John at the Southern Shore Music Festival,
Millville, NJ, June 21, 2008

Foreword

Art wuz the mos' slammin', jammin', fantastic bombastic drummer in the galaxy. He could start the chart off, burn it, turnin' it into somethin' cookin', never overlookin' nuttin'.

On all those classic Blue Note sessions with Monk, Miles, and Horace, according to the likes of Earl Palmer, he was the "wu," talkin' 'bout the Bu. In fac', I thought on Monk's "Bye-Ya" that they wuz from New Orleans. It felt so much part of my roots.

Lemme pull yo coat to how I met Art Blakey. My old lady at the time, Cozette, had a hideaway that so happen' to be behind Art's crib. I didn't have the key to Cozette's.

Walter Davis said, "I can git you into Cozette's pad," when he called me from Art's place.

Well, I got in and tiptoed through Art's abode till I kicked over a metal pail. When I looked up, Art's 9 mm wuz starin' me in the face. That's how I met Bu, and his daughter Evelyn never let me forget it. Art was cool to lemme through anyhow after Walter explained I was a musician and would "tighten him up later".

Meetin' Sandy wuz as unexpected as meetin' Bu, but I wuzn't sneakin' and she wuzn't packin'.

I'm hangin' out in front of the bus at the Millville, NJ fairgrounds waitin' to go on at this little music festival. The pocket calendar says it's the first night of summer, 2008. People's comin' over to talk and git pictures taken.

Everything wuz pretty ordinary. Then, all of a sudden – pow! – I felt a pair of eyeballs goin' hellbent through me and landin' someplace in my soul. I looked around and they wuz comin' from this little bitty blonde with a yellow flower in her hair way in the back o' the crowd. I don't remember exactly what I did next, but she said I parted the seas and made way for her to come to the front. To me a person's eyeballs is the door to their soul. If you ain't got good eyeballs, I ain't got time for ya.

Her eyeballs never changed direction. She walked right up smilin' that smile, stood on her tiptoes, put her arms around me, and kissed me on the forehead. She looked me hard in the eyes and said almos' whisperin', "I'm Art Blakey's Sandy."

Damn! I started grinnin' and tellin' her how I met Bu. She said she wanted to do somethin' more to help New Orleans, a book or somethin'. She wanted to donate some of the profits.

We ain't stopped talkin' yet; don't think we will on this planet or the next. Her big ol' brown eyeballs are an immovable fixture in my soul and that's as good as it gits in this life.

Now, about this book yer lookin' at. Bu was a musician's musician. Hell, he still is. No squabblin' about that. But he was also Sandy's love and Takashi's pop, and that's what it's all about.

It ain't no tell-all biography, discography, or fictitious

Hollywood movie script by somebody who didn't even know him. It's the sweet 'n sour story of a woman and her man makin' a home together, raisin' a son, and havin' a ball cookin' up a hell of a storm. Yea, it's a simmerin' good gumbo.

It don't matter whether you're a jazz fan, a good cook, a bad cook, or no cook at all. If you got feelin's, there's somethin' in this tasty bowl of a book for ya. So lean back and listen.

Mac Rebennack

(Dr. John)

December, 2009

Photo by Hans Harzheim, Duesseldorf, Germany

Takashi and Art on tour in Germany.

PROLOGUE

Note on the Kitchen Table

*There is no gift more special than the memory
of a good meal with people we love. Our
culinary traditions and the stories embracing
them are so powerful they outweigh nearly
everything else in our memory banks.*

Anonymous

Dear Takashi and Beth,

Here's the family recipe collection I promised
you for a wedding gift.

I know you weren't expecting a bound book. I
wasn't either. It all started out simply enough. I
transcribed some recipes by hand on 4x6 cards and
dutifully placed them in the proper food categories
of a pretty floral recipe box. Then the next thing
I knew I was writing recollections on the cards,
sometimes even having to staple a second or third
card onto the original. Things continued to get out
of hand, and before I knew it, the recipe collection
had become the size of a book probably best
described as a culinary memoir. And what's a book
about cookin' and jammin' with Art without some
pictures? For you, dear Takashi, it is a gift of legacy
and heritage. For Beth, it's a look at life with the

father-in-law you never met, a chance to know the extraordinary man Takashi simply called Pop.

Finally, this remembrance is also for friends and others we never knew whose days and nights were kicked up a notch or two by Art's zest for living and for all those foodies whose favorite room is the kitchen.

In love and wonder,

Sandy

Addendum:

While this book was in progress, Layla Hana Blakey was born to Beth and Takashi on September 15, 2006. Layla, may this book be a loving link to your granddad who would have adored you.

Kaden William Blakey was born February 10, 2009. Kaden, I hope this memoir takes you on a great adventure with your granddad whose loving spirit watches over you.

CONTENTS

Takashi with his foodie aunt, Jane Retter (Keener).

Layla, age six months, gearing up for her first jazz fest
honoring her Granddad Art.

Introduction

Heart Walker

If the dead be truly dead, why should they still be walking in my heart?

Shoshone Medicine Man

The person who influenced my life most profoundly is Art Blakey. Period. Twenty years after his death, he still strides through my heart.

Long before cancer destroyed him with so much vengeance, Art asked me to write his biography. He reminisced on planes, in bed, at the kitchen table, on the toilet, and I took notes. When he died in 1990, so did my will to finish the book.

Then finally somewhere along the line, I realized I was lugging around in my mind the jumbled fragments of this cookbook-memoir and I began to sort out the pieces and put them on paper. *Art Blakey Cookin' and Jammin'* is a very personal account of life with Art told in recipes and remembrances. It's a celebration of the time we had together – a piece of twine that binds past, present, and future but not without the pain of an occasional rope burn.

I believe that every life, irrespective of its events
and setting, holds something of unique value which
it should be possible to communicate, if only one
can first see one's experiences honestly and then
set them down without too much dressing-up.

Iris Origo

On these pages, I have tried to show there was more to
Art than the grinning, boisterous genius behind the drums.
There was a complicated being of extreme contradictions
who had more to do with the person I have become than
my mother and father. I will carry with me forever the
things I learned from this sometimes gentle man who col-
lected dolls and displayed them in an antique case in our
living room. This is the same man who flew into a rage and
threatened to have one of his own sons arrested for charg-
ing a hundred dollars worth of calls to our phone bill.

His personality was so powerful that he could charm
strangers into giving him money which usually went for
heroin and car washes – in that order. Whether he was
driving an old or new Cadillac, he liked to keep it clean.

At home, having found all the cash I'd carefully hidden
in books and record jackets, he'd leave to buy a pack of
cigarettes and days later return disheveled, bearing yet
another potted plant he'd picked up on credit from the
florist down the block. Then he'd take a shower, get the car
washed and waxed, put his arm around me and break into

a big grin and announce, "Egghead, let's go to New Orleans and eat some drunken shrimp." That was code for "Let's go down the road to Tull's and fill up on shrimp, lobster, flounder or whatever else makes you happy. I missed you girl."

I'd smile right back and race him to the car. He wasn't a fast runner. Even with my short strides, I always beat him.

Somebody said great musicians are never normal people. He must have run into Art at the cigarette counter.

Photo courtesy of Beth Blakey

Takashi Buhaina Blakey on the day he was born,
October 31, 1969, the day that all our lives were
transformed forever for the better.

Roots and Bootstraps

Into each of our lives there steps a magical person… They stir our pots; they ruffle our feathers. They paste twinkling stars on the dark night sky.

Daphne Rose Kingma, Author

It is said that people tell their life stories through food and music. Simmering a pot of chili spiced just right and serving it to someone we love nurtures us in the deepest recesses of our soul just as surely as a "Blues March" drum solo does.

If you're lucky, once in a lifetime, somebody comes along and shares with you an unbounded passion for both food and music and you are forever changed. It happened to me on a Tuesday night in August, 1968, when I was 28, at Slug's, a jazz club in New York City's East Village. That's when I met Art. My friend Myrna and I had gone to this hole-in-the-wall joint, which consistently booked the best jazz artists, just to hear one set. Don Underwood, who booked gigs for the Somers Point (New Jersey) Jazz Society, described Slug's this way: "Go and soak up the best jazz on the planet. Just don't drink out of the glasses 'cause they may not have been soaked, at least not in hot water. And don't go out the front door looking to flag down a cab after the set. The cabs don't cruise around here."

Anyway, the whole band with the master on drums was

cookin': Ronnie Matthews, piano; Lawrence Evans, bass; Bill Hardman, trumpet; Julian Priester, trombone; and Billy Harper, tenor sax. Without even planning to, we stayed till closing. Afterwards, I went up to thank Art. He was so touched by that simple gesture he invited us to come back as his guests the following night. Short on money and impressed with his genuine graciousness, I immediately accepted for both Myrna and myself.

He was between wives, lovers, new Cadillacs, wardrobes, record contracts, bank accounts and apartments and it showed. Heroin had robbed him of just about everything except his abundance of talent and charm. Nothing and nobody could ever take those.

At the club Wednesday night, he flirted with me during the breaks and just before the last set, followed me into the women's restroom, locked the door, and kissed me. It felt good, and I kissed him back. Afterwards he just smiled that smile that I would never tire of.

The second question people ask me after "Where did you meet Art?" is "What attracted you to him?" Those who know me have already eliminated my being a groupie, doper, or gold digger. I admit some things are impossible even for writers to fully express. But I'll give it a go.

I've believed in love at first sight since I was a teenager. With Art, I'd say it was love at second sight in Detroit about a month after we first met at Slug's. Starting that first night and building over time, there were things that drew me to him that made me like and then love him: the explosive, uncensored sharing of his God given musical talent, the special smile, the way he made me feel at ease, an attentiveness to things I said and did, the sense of humor and mischief, the openness, being so down to earth and approachable. As I write, I'm reminded these are qualities I'd respond to in anybody.

Trying to analyze the chemistry – what made my heart pound and put the butterflies in my stomach – doesn't really need dwelling on at all because we've all felt it sometime about somebody.

I said I admired his openness and that included his being up front about the dark side of heroin addiction. I learned quickly that getting dope would almost always take precedence over all else except his music.

The first place he took me in the wee hours of Thursday morning was to his dealer's apartment. When he was using, which was off and on throughout his life, he always needed a fix after a gig. Wednesday night into Thursday morning was no exception. It was one of many late nights I would sit uneasily in a stranger's living room waiting for Art to come out of the bedroom or bathroom, having shared a needle with some other users. Sometimes he knew them; sometimes he didn't.

I never had second thoughts or regrets about loving a man who was an addict. That's hard to explain to somebody who's never loved a junkie, but that's how it was. I loved the person, not the shit he shot into his veins.

The second thing we did was drive past Monk's apartment building. Art idolized Thelonious Sphere Monk. At 5:00 a.m. on a Thursday even Manhattan was almost quiet as we slowly passed the nondescript brick building at 243 West 63rd Street where this extraordinary pianist lived. Later I would travel with Art and Monk on the Giants of Jazz Tour and begin to understand the endless bond between these two exceptional men. For the time being, I had to be content just going past Monk's home.

Art's love and admiration for Monk were apparent to all who saw them together or, for that matter, anybody who ever spent even a bit of time with Art. He was on Monk's first recording for Blue Note in 1947. And he was there in 1971 when Monk recorded his last trio for Black Lion Records in London. They were true soul mates whose birthdays were only a day apart. Art was born October 11, 1919 and Monk on October 10, 1917.

Friday and Saturday flew by quickly and at sunup Sunday morning, Art gave me a kiss and a bear hug and dropped me off in front of the 34th Street YMCA, a cheap hotel of miniscule, oppressively hot rooms with toilets at the end of the hall. The whole place reeked with the smell of urine.

In a way, though, I was grateful to be getting out of the car there. Even at its worst, it was better than the Albert Hotel in the Village, where I'd spent my first days in an unlocked room because the manager couldn't find a key for the door. Not nearly as many of my fellow travelers at the Y were having noisy LSD trips at all hours either. The Albert must have been resting on its laurels or maybe even been passed out on them. It had no resemblance to the hotel of "Rear Window" fame where Jimmy Stewart asked Raymond Burr to meet for a drink in the bar.

Neither Art nor I were good at farewells so we kept them short from the beginning. As I walked away from the car, Art called out "Be safe, Egghead. We'll go eat shrimp when I get back, New Orleans shrimp." I turned and smiled and told him to have a good tour. He had given me a nickname and I liked it. A pet name is a sign of closeness. And I didn't mind being thought of as brainy. I also liked that he remembered shrimp was one of my favorite foods and New Orleans one of my favorite places.

The Japan tour meant a lot to Art. The band was always paid better there than anywhere else in the world. Venues were good, pianos were tuned, and fans were adoring.

Inside the Y, I went up in the creaky elevator and immediately said a prayer of thanks when the door opened on the 12th floor. Hastily, I packed my small soft-sided blue plaid carry-on bag to go home to Chicago with Myrna. Art went I don't know where and packed his large vinyl tan bag for Asia. He didn't have much to put in it. The only outfits he'd worn all week were a few dashikis with matching poorly tailored pants that were too short and appeared to have been sewn as an afterthought from leftover drapery material. With temperatures in New York in the 90s, they must have been unbearable. Art should have been able to afford clothing crafted from the best authentic African cloth. In New York any fabric you would want was available. It saddened me because I knew he loved Africa and its culture, having lived there in the 1940s. I hoped that his habit would not eat up his tour profits and he'd be able to buy some new finer things when he returned.

I also hoped when he got back to New York, he'd get a

permanent room or maybe even an apartment with a telephone. Then he wouldn't have to pretend anymore that he owned an imposing red brick house on Staten Island where he invited me to take up residence, but never gave me the address. Maybe he could even get his clunky old Cadillac repaired so it could go all the way from the Village to Midtown without conking out. Yes, the Japanese tour could make a lot of things happen.

A month went quickly. I returned to work, as a counselor at what became Kennedy King College, but back then was still Wilson Campus of the City Colleges of Chicago. This only slightly converted warehouse on the south side of 71st and Wentworth was a microcosm of 1960s society. The majority of students at the two-year institution were poor blacks who arrived daily by foot on the 69th Street cross town bus. They were seriously seeking the tools to pursue careers mostly in business, social services, or education. Dedicated activist faculty members willingly committed their talents to helping them accomplish their goals. I still hold tightly to and treasure some of my faculty friendships 40 years later.

Then there were some exceptions, like the tenured music professor who informed me blacks couldn't read music. I dropped off some of my Ellington vinyls among others for his enlightenment, but the ones who educated him the most were his own proficient black students.

On a chilly Friday night in late September, I caught a flight to Detroit and checked in at the downtown Sheraton. I didn't know where Art was staying and didn't want to seem presumptuous or pushy, anyway. After all, my showing up was sort of a surprise. We hadn't made any definite plans. But I think he knew I'd be there for his first gig back in the States. As I strode into Baker's Keyboard Lounge and headed for the empty front-row-center table, Art eyed me. He smiled that infectious broad smile and nodded. When the tune ended, he quickly jumped up to the mike. "This next one's for my lady, Egghead," he announced, and the band began "It's Only a Paper Moon."

It's only a paper moon sailing over a cardboard sea.

But it wouldn't be make believe if you believed in me.

(music by Harold Arlen,
lyrics by E.Y. [Yip] Harburg)

Through the years, he would introduce me to audiences all over North America and Europe and would dedicate many songs to me, but none would mean more than this first one.

Every once in a while, I still repeat the lyrics to myself and smile.

After the gig and burgers and fries at an all night coffee shop, Art sent his Detroit buddy, Jerry, to move my things out of the Sheraton and into his motel room.

Meantime, my friend Gloria, who had joined me at the club, gave me a hug, proclaimed Art was a keeper, and headed back to Ann Arbor, fully convinced I was in good hands.

The motel was one of those basic 1950s plastic/vinyl structures that clogged Woodward Ave. We propped all the pillows up against the brown veneer headboard and sat on the bed talking all night about the past and present. Some other time we'd dare speak of the future.

I began learning about this complicated man's birth and upbringing, so different from mine. About the only thing we shared in common was being an only child. Oh, yes there was one more: both of us were fathered by handsome barbers. That's where the similarities stopped. I was nurtured by my young parents, Paul and Maxine, plus Granny Green, Grandma Warren, Aunt Jessie and Uncle Buster as well as a slew of other relatives, caring teachers and neighbors. Art had only an overburdened Sara Perran. I thrived in my small town of Winchester, Indiana, while he did the best he could to survive the grit and racism of 1920s and 30s Pittsburgh.

Art's father was Bertram T. Blakey, a tall, self-involved, slightly built handsome man of light skin from Pittsburgh's Hill District. In contrast, his young mother, Marie Jackson Blakey was plain, short, dark, shy and in love. Shortly before Art was delivered by a midwife on October 11, 1919, his parents married and departed the ceremony in the same buggy in which the child had been conceived. Bertram pulled up in front of the neighborhood smoke shop and went in for a cigar. He got his stogie and left by the back door, never to see his wife again. Weary and melancholy, she died when Art was an infant. Some said her cause of death was a broken heart. Art first met his father at the funeral home.

Bertram Blakey and his family refused to claim the dark-skinned baby with Negroid features who bore little resemblance to them. Art, who had been named James

Edward, was taken in and raised by his mother's cousin, Sara Perran, who had children of her own and worked as a domestic. Her husband had threatened to leave her if she brought home another mouth to feed. She came in carrying Art, and true to his word, he walked out the door.

As a tribute to his mother, Art on stage referred to himself as Mrs. Blakey's one and only son, but he always remained grateful to Sara Perran for giving him the home his natural mother couldn't. Looking back now, I think Art got a lot of his strong will and toughness from Sara. It took both, plus God-given talent, to go from seventh grade dropout to world's greatest jazz drummer without ever having a music lesson. Along the way, he would compose and coauthor numerous tunes and lead the Jazz Messengers unerringly for 35 years.

In Detroit, we started a ritual we'd repeat everywhere we went. We bought flowers and brought them back to the room, where we stuck them in empty wine bottles, plastic cups, and whatever else we could find. The blossoms transformed the room and made the impersonal space ours. They marked our territory. Life was grand.

I went home to Chicago reluctantly Monday but was right back again on Friday for another long weekend. Art rented a red Mustang, and we took leisurely drives in the country. The leaves were already beginning to turn but the afternoons were still warm. This was a far cry from clunking around the pot holed streets of Manhattan in a broken-down old Caddie. I thrived on the ease with which we spent our days and nights together and revealed ourselves to one another.

I learned that Art's next meeting with B.T., which is what everyone called Bertram Blakey, was in the barbershop. Now six years old, cold, and hungry, he went into the shop just to beg a few pennies for some candy and to get warm. Art would remember B.T.'s loud cutting reply for the rest of his life. Glaring down on the small, barefooted child, he said, "I wouldn't piss in your ear if your brains was on fire, boy. Now get outta here." The man Art would bury on another cold, bleak day 51 years later was a stranger, a father in name only.

When he was 13, Art left Herron Junior High to work full time. He took whatever menial day jobs he could get, from making steel in sweltering mills to digging graves. At night, he and his small band played local Mafia-owned clubs. Later on he would become proficient at reading music. But as a young teenage piano player, he would memorize tunes by simply hearing the band run through them once.

Then one afternoon, the club owner gave them a new tune he wanted to hear that same night. Art didn't get it down even after the second run-through. The owner said, "I'll bet the kid over there in the corner could do a better job than you, Blakey. Hey, kid, come here and play the piano. Blakey, you take over the drums." The quiet kid came across the room and sat down at the piano, where he played the song effortlessly.

The beaming owner said, "Kid, what's your name? You're hired."

"Errol Garner," the young man answered.

Walking back to the bar, the owner added, "You weren't so bad on the drums either, Blakey."

By 1939, Art, then 20, had put together enough money for the move to New York, where he washed dishes by day and by night made the rounds of jazz clubs seeking work. His break came when he got a gig in Fletcher Henderson's reorganized band. That was all he needed. He would go on to change the history of jazz and drumming. No longer would the drummer be relegated strictly to timekeeper.

He was the drummer in Billy Eckstine's big band from 1944 to 1947. Propelled by Art's drive and the creativity of Bird, Dizzy, Monk and Miles, this group could do no wrong.

Alfred Lion, who founded Blue Note Records, took notice and made Art his house drummer.

During the Eckstine years was when Art forged an unbreakable bond with New Orleans that endured the rest of his life.

According to New Orleans drummer Vernel Fournier, the Eckstine band came to town every few months. He recalled going to see them when he was only fourteen or fifteen and credited Art with being his first bebop influence. "Once I heard Art Blakey, it cancelled out everything,"

Earl Palmer put it this way in *Modern Drummer*, May, 1983: "I got out of the service December 10, 1945, and the following week I went to a concert where Billy Eckstine's band was playing and the local band that played before them was Dooky Chase. Vernel Fournier was playing drums in Dooky's band and Art Blakey was with Billy Eckstine's band. I heard both those drummers that night and said, 'That's it. I'm going to play drums.'"

Art was an emotional man whose highs were reflected in his soulful hard-bop style. Saxophonist Ike Quebec described it: "Other drummers say thump, Blakey says POW." Art formed the Jazz Messengers quintet with Horace Silver in 1954. A year later Horace split and Art became sole leader of this historic funky group for the next 35 years.

In *Jazz Portraits*, Len Lyons and Don Perlo observed, "The leader's long press roll followed by a cymbal crash seems to elevate the entire band a foot or two above the stage." I can only add that it did the same thing to the audience. Art's drumming always could bring me to my feet and my knees and give me both smiles and tears within the same tune, no matter how many times I'd heard it.

Photo by Lee Tanner

Thelonious Sphere Monk up close in this photo just as
he was up close in Art's life. Thank you, Lee, for gifting
me with this priceless image.

Photo courtesy of The Michael P. Smith Archive at The Historic New Orleans Collection

Art appearing at the '72 New Orleans Jazz Fest
with the Giants of Jazz.

Journey to a Sunny Kitchen

Love is a beautiful journey but the road can be bumpy and slow.

Daphne Rose Kingma, Author

I flew out of Detroit on that September 1968 morning, knowing I'd see Art again soon. His 49th birthday was coming up and Marlene Stokes, saxophonist Billy Harper's girlfriend, and I had already planned a bash. She'd get a giant cake inscribed "Love Bu" - Bu was a nickname good friends had given Art years ago when he returned from Africa having taken the Muslim name Abdullah Ibn Buhaina. I'd show up and surprise Art at the club. I remember everything about that night except the name of the club, which has long since gone kaput.

My friend Chick Wilson, who taught me more about jazz than anybody else and was now living in Connecticut, eagerly agreed to pick me up at the airport and whisk me to the gig. Believe me, when Chick took you someplace, he whisked you there. He knew how to weave and whiz through traffic even on a Friday night in Manhattan.

It was one of those perfect evenings. We got there just as the first set was starting and Art looked over with that irrepressible big smile. At the end of the set, the club owner got on the mike and invited everybody to gather 'round the bar. While Marlene lit the candles, I grabbed Art's hand and led him behind the bar. Everybody sang

"Happy Birthday" as he blew them out. I quietly wondered if he'd make a wish and what it was. All I knew is that he was so surprised and touched that he had tears in his eyes. It was one of the few times I would ever see that.

"Egghead, this is the best birthday I've ever had," he said as he squeezed my hand. Just nine words from a usually talkative man, but it was all I needed to hear.

On the way to the airport Sunday night, my cab was involved in an accident and I missed the red-eye. I took it as a sign to return to the Mansfield Hotel, awaken Art, and stay another ten days.

Autumn in New York is everything the Vernon Duke song says it is, but autumn in London, Paris, and Amsterdam is more lucrative for jazz bands. So the Messengers headed off to Europe, returning home just before Thanksgiving. Their European concerts and club dates always were well received, and this tour was no exception.

Marlene took off work, and we met the arriving plane. Billy was grinning from ear to ear when he saw Marlene, but that turned quickly to a look of uneasiness when he spotted me. He sputtered that Art hadn't come back with the guys but would definitely be in on the same flight tomorrow because they had a concert at NYU that night. He was so uncomfortable that I didn't have the heart to ask any questions.

Sure enough, Art came striding through customs Saturday afternoon just as Billy said he would. What Billy hadn't told me was that another woman would be with him. My mouth went dry. I was shaking. The only noise I could hear was the deafening pounding of my heart. I still don't know how I managed to put one foot in front of the other and make my way toward the man in my life and the mystery woman in his.

Art spied me, let go of her hand, and waved. He broke into that broad smile that had greeted me so many times in the last few months. I smiled back and quickened my pace. My legs and feet had suddenly become steady and my throat irrigated. I became aware of the sounds around me – families and friends reuniting, luggage being dragged, announcements from the PA system … Most of all, I could hear Art calling, "Egghead." I ran right into his arms, which tightened around me. For a long moment, he was my whole world.

When I once again became conscious of my surroundings and looked over at his companion, her blank expression had not changed. Politely, but with no show of emotion, Art said, "Sandy, this is Atsuko." I, in turn, with no particular show of emotion, made eye contact with her and simply said, "Hello." She nodded. Art quickly changed the focus from introductions to the more pressing need at hand, saying, "Let's get a taxi."

On the trip into the City, Art sat between us, and he and I caught up on each other's lives over the past several weeks. The only thing he neglected to mention was where Atsuko fit into the picture. She remained expressionless and silent on the whole ride.

"I'll tell you about her later," Art said before dropping me off at Marlene's. "Come to the NYU gig tonight."

"I will," I assured him as I kissed him on the cheek.

The concert was upbeat, crowded, and loud, an appropriate homecoming for the Messengers. Still, I found my eyes stealing away from the band and focusing on Atsuko more than I had anticipated. I was guiltily doing a mental checklist, a comparison of this quiet woman in the corner. Her short, dark, straight hair was in place. My short, naturally curly, blonde hair looked wind-blown. Her clear, fair complexion was in contrast to my rougher, slightly tanned skin. We were both short, just less than 5 feet, and slim. I held the trump card in the wardrobe department. I was wearing the brown wool bell-bottoms and beige cashmere sweater Art had bought me on my last trip to the City. Atsuko had on an ill-fitting polyester floral dress. The comparisons were petty, yet I kept dwelling on them.

After the first set, Art took me into a suffocatingly tiny room down the hall. His demeanor was more serious than usual. "Egghead, I didn't tell you about Atsuko because I didn't want to risk losing you. You know my daughter Evelyn went with the band to Japan as the vocalist. She'd gone with us before and she and Atsuko had become friends. Then the next thing I knew, Atsuko and I were spending time together, day and night. She didn't speak much English, but she was a big fan and easy to be with. She fell in love and wanted me to bring her to America. Evelyn kept pestering me about it, too. After all, I was divorced and not seriously involved with anybody. And, like I said, she was easy to be with. So finally I said yes, on the next trip, I'd bring her to the U.S. and look after her."

"Hell, I didn't know I was going to meet you a few days

before I went to Japan for the tour. Then I couldn't figure out how to tell you the promise I'd made her. You're the best part of my life besides those drums." He pulled me toward him. "Now you know, and I still don't want to lose you."

Didn't he know my leaving wasn't even an option? Our lives were already so emotionally intertwined nothing could pull us apart.

The band started the next set with "Moanin'." I still have every recording of it the Messengers ever made.

Art and I continued to make a home on the road while he and Atsuko made a home in New York. Atsuko was little more than an inconvenience and an irritant. She had a habit of screaming "No!" and hanging up whenever I called their apartment, but I really couldn't blame her.

Then in the spring of 1969, everything changed. Art and Atsuko hadn't shared much of a life but they did share a bed. On a cold, windy March afternoon, Atsuko, not feeling well, walked over to the emergency room at Roosevelt Hospital, where she learned she was pregnant. When she came home and told Art, there was no talk of abortion. They would raise this child together somehow. They would find space in that small one-bedroom Times Square apartment. On October 31, 1969, a life altering event would affect us all for the better forever. Takashi Ibn Buhaina was born healthy but two months premature. Atsuko gave birth alone. Art was on a gig. In December, Art married her in a civil ceremony at city hall because he felt strongly it was the right thing to do. Call us old-fashioned, but I, too, felt it was right.

Isolated and overwhelmed, she was ill-equipped for motherhood. She had not had time to learn a new language, make friends, or assimilate into the culture. Life was difficult and uncertain. Art, on the other hand, thrived on parenthood. He was both mother and father to Takashi. Between out-of-town bookings, they were inseparable. They paddled boats in Central Park, circled Washington Square on foot, and rode the A train to Harlem. They even went to gigs together. This beautiful toddler attended the first Newport in New York Festival in July, 1972, when he was two. While the rest of us jammed out front, Takashi, with his olive skin and ringlets of soft black hair, sat cross legged backstage, never taking his brown eyes off his father's motions.

Art even took Atsuko and Takashi on the road with him when it was feasible. The rest of the time, I joined him as often as I could.

As I'm reminiscing and writing this, Hurricane Katrina's wrath is still raw and fresh in my head. But I'm also thinking back to the early 1970s and that glorious springtime ritual, the New Orleans Jazz and Heritage Festival. One of the things that impressed me most, besides the affordable tickets, was the way George and Joyce Wein treated the musicians, whom they housed in the *grand dame* of the French Quarter, the Royal Sonesta, where champagne, chocolate on the pillows, and fruit baskets were standard. Limousines ferried the jazz greats to and from their venues.

Wein has always had a keen sense of history and a knack for putting the right geniuses together in the right space at the right time. On Saturday, April 29, 1972, at 8:00 p.m. the Giants of Jazz played to a cheering on their feet audience at the third Jazz Fest. The energy flowing back and forth among them and Art (drums), Monk (piano), Dizzy (trumpet), Kai Winding (trombone), Sonny Stitt (sax), and Al McKibbon (bass) was incredible. I had tears running down my cheeks and a big grin on my face at the same time. What a historic night.

Both George and Joyce were down to earth and didn't pull rank. They jumped in wherever they were needed. When Art had to get back to New York right after his Sunday gig, Joyce drove him to the airport. She invited me to ride along and I did. George, if you're reading this, you were sooo lucky to have her all those years, but you already know that.

And one more thing, George … If you ever make a list of the jazz accomplishments you're most proud of, I think those Giants tours will be in bold letters at the top o' the page. As you said in the liner notes on their record, it was a great adventure. And a great adventure it still is. I'm playing the album now as I write this. Timeless.

I consider myself one of the luckiest people on the planet to have been on the European leg of this invaluable piece of jazz history. My most poignant memory involves Monk who had gone into a period of self-imposed silence. Nellie, his wife, was doing the talking for the both of them. Anyway, every night when the car would come to take us to the gig, Monk, dressed splendidly in a suit and tie, would be seated in the back seat. Then when I got in, he'd smile, greet me, and tell me how pretty I looked. And that would be the extent of his worldly conversation for the next 24 hours. I remain in awe to have been the recipient of his contact no matter how brief. I never knew why Monk withdrew into himself. I simply respected his privacy.

I'm smiling now as I think about the entertainer at a Bourbon Street bar I didn't expect to see, an authentic flamenco dancer. I was mesmerized by her then and still love the dance today. That's the way it was with Art, always something unexpected around the next corner.

One of those unexpected things came in the form of a life-altering phone call from Art in January, 1973. Atusko had told him she and Takashi would accompany him on the band's upcoming trip to Japan, but that she would not return to the States. Art could keep Takashi. She wouldn't try to raise him in Japan where interracial children were considered outcasts.

"Egghead, pack your trunk. I want you to come to New York and make a home with Takashi and me."

My heart was pounding so loudly I thought it would drown out my words. In a stream of tears, I managed to say something less than profound. "Oh, my God, yes."

After I shakily hung up the phone, my mind went in a zillion directions. I recalled that when I was a second grader, my favorite teacher, Miss Hart, asked us what we wanted to be when we grew up. I proudly proclaimed that I wanted to be three things: a New Yorker forever; a teacher during the school year; and circus performer in the summer. Twenty-four years later I would realize one-third of that dream. The other two-thirds no longer mattered. I was going to be a New Yorker. I would be home, at last, sharing my life with the two people I loved most.

I arrived at LaGuardia with ten suitcases, including the matching tan Samsonite set my old boyfriend Scotty had given me for high school graduation. Art, already in Japan, sent a uniformed chauffeur in a Cadillac limousine to meet me.

At the end of the Japan tour, the band's itinerary was to land in Chicago and go straight to the gig at Joe Segel's Jazz Showcase on Rush Street. I knew the club well. It was just steps from where I had lived in Delaware Towers.

After getting temporarily settled in a dismal women-only hotel in New York, I backtracked to Chicago to hook up with Art and Takashi at the club. They were already there when I arrived. While Art was busy setting up, Takashi was freely running around the room speaking Japanese. I dashed over, scooped him up, and showered him with kisses. Art saw us and joined the welcome party.

It was a festive, high-energy night. Joe's clubs and sessions always drew the most knowledgeable jazz fans. Takashi didn't even take time out for his usual nap back-stage. After the last set, the three of us left the club arm in arm heading up Rush Street, laughing and talking all at once. We hadn't gone more than half a block when I felt a blow to the back of my head. I screamed and my knees started to buckle. All three of us swung around at the same time. Atsuko was right behind me, carrying the black vinyl purse she had hit me with, and was shouting at me to go back where I came from. Art snapped her name loudly, took her arm forcefully, and escorted her across the street to the hotel while Takashi and I increased our grip on one another and waited on the sidewalk. I felt like I was going to throw up, and would have if I hadn't been too excited to eat all day. The woman I thought was living in Japan was here in Chicago claiming her husband and son, and she had every right to do so.

After a few minutes, Art returned. He looked stern and detached. Without even making eye contact, he said, "She just changed her mind about staying in Japan. That's all."

Logic told me I should end the self-destructive path I was on right then and there. I was less than a block from my old apartment building. They almost always had furnished efficiencies for rent. Maybe I could have even gotten my one-bedroom on the third floor again, and I would have been welcomed back to work at Kennedy-King College. But I wasn't operating on logic. I was on raw emotion, and that trumps logic every time. So instead of staying in Chicago, I took a flight to New York while the Messengers, with Takashi and Atsuko, went on to St. Louis. I moved my stuff in a cab to a one-room furnished apartment at the Roger Williams on 29th at Madison, a staid and worn red brick building housing elderly single residents, who were a pretty good match for the building's appearance. I rented it primarily for the balcony that stretched the entire length of the 13th floor room. To say the Manhattan view was spectacular would be an understatement. The kitchen consisted of a two-burner hot plate, tiny sink, and a mini fridge.

When he wasn't on the road, Art divided his time between the Camelot, where he lived with Atsuko, and the Roger Williams on no particular schedule. He'd bring Takashi over to live with me when Atsuko was too ill to care for him and take him back each time she was a bit better. The roller coaster ride took its toll. Every time Takashi was pulled away, I got more depressed. Clinical depression and suicidal thoughts haunted me and there was nowhere to turn. Free counseling services were scarce and waiting lists were long.

I realized that whenever Takashi was wrenched from me, I was reliving the still raw wounds of October 18, 1961, the morning I surrendered my one-day-old son, Tim, for adoption in Indianapolis. With no family or community support, I had been told the most loving thing I could do was allow a good family to raise him. The two of us would not be reunited until Valentine's Day, 2006.

When Takashi was with Atsuko, I'd replay in my mind the everyday things we'd done together that were so joyful – taking long walks and stopping for ice cream (vanilla for him, chocolate for me), shopping for trinkets at the variety store, checking out storybooks at the Kips Bay Branch of the library - even doing laundry was fun when we did it together. Takashi was always up for going out to eat lunch or dinner. There were lots of inexpensive neighborhood restaurants nearby. We feasted on pepperoni pizza, Chinese beef with green peppers and onions, chicken and noodles, and more.

Art paid the rent, but I still needed money for food and other expenses. So I took a part-time job as a rent collector in a SRO (single room occupancy) red brick building at 27 West 11th Street in the Village. Today, all gussied up, it's a boutique hotel called the Larchmont.

I suppose I would have kept settling indefinitely for half a life on this amusement ride to nowhere if Art had kept up the rent. Then it happened. On a sunny early October afternoon, I went out alone to get a few groceries. When I returned, there was a plug in the door lock. The manager matter-of-factly said it would stay there until the two weeks back rent was paid, along with a week's rent in advance. Meantime, all my stuff would be moved to a locked storage room in the basement. In a shaky voice, almost a whisper, I pleaded with him to unlock the door long enough for me to retrieve Freckles, my black and white cocker spaniel. He agreed. I rushed in and also quickly grabbed the leash, wicker carrying case, and a couple of dog burgers along with a sweater and clean underwear for myself.

I called Art from the nearest pay phone. "I'll be right over, baby. Meet me in front of the coffee shop on the corner, and we'll get this straightened out."

This was the last time I would speak to him and let him know my whereabouts for a year. With Freckles in tow, I waited on the corner two hours. I vacillated between visualizing him pulling up in a Checker Cab and rescuing me to leaving me on the street to fend for myself. After all, he was a heroin addict, and as with all addicts, heroin came first. Art's relationship with the needle could make other relationships unimportant. I was shivering as I made my way across town to the West 50s to seek refuge at Marlene's. She and I had remained friends even after she and

Billy Harper had broken up. She could have said, "I told you so." She didn't.

After a frantic phone call, Jane Retter, my best friend, who'd left Manhattan for Montclair, New Jersey, to live with percussionist Lawrence Killian, borrowed Lawrence's car and came for Freckles and me. I spent a restless night on Jane's couch and prayed somebody would spot Art tomorrow. But by the next night, he was still nowhere to be found. His booking agent, Jack Whittemore, took pity on me and paid the back rent and said he would collect from Art later. I loaded what clothes, records, and books I could into a taxi and put them in storage at the Sheraton baggage room.

Jack paid for the room on one condition – that I leave Art. He didn't see things improving anytime soon. I knew he was right but it hurt to admit it. I also knew it meant disappearing from New York with no forwarding address because Art's pull on me was so great.

I reluctantly agreed, and after a few phone calls, with $25 in my pocket, I was on the bus to Atlantic City, where I'd take a counseling job at Atlantic Community College. Jane, the only one who knew my destination, kept it a secret. In the next year, she would leave Lawrence and join me there.

I checked into one of those cheap 1950s motels that lined Pacific Avenue, after convincing the motel manager to accept my rent check dated two weeks in advance. The room was clean, no mice and no roaches, and had cooking facilities.

Next thing I did was buy a jar of peanut butter and a loaf of Wonder Bread. That would be lunch until my first pay check. I don't recall buying anything for dinner except a bag of Red Delicious apples. What I mostly remember was missing Takashi so much that I wasn't hungry anyway.

I was miserable and fantasized about staying just long enough to collect a paycheck and head back to New York, where everything would magically work out. Sometimes you have to be careful what you wish for because it might come true. Luckily for me, my hopes were not realized. Going right back to the City would have been yet another act of self-destruction.

The Atlantic City boardwalk saved me. It was my therapy. When I got blisters on my feet, I simply bandaged them and walked some more.

Weeks turned into months and I eventually made friends, found an apartment just steps from the ocean, and settled into a love-hate relationship with my job.

In August 1974, an ad appeared in the Philadelphia Inquirer touting the Messengers' upcoming gig at a local club. I felt emotionally strong enough to go, not on the first night, but later in the week. My neighbor, Harriet Feldman, and I quietly slipped in about halfway through the first set so I had time to steady myself before Art even noticed us. Looking back, I really don't know exactly what I expected. In fact, I don't remember much about the whole week. I do recall that when the evening ended, I agreed to come back the next night and stay the weekend, repeating a familiar pattern. It felt natural to be with Art, taking up where we left off. I was home where I was supposed to be.

I also remember that Art and Harriet hit it off well and he talked her into coming with me to the upcoming Boston gig. We all had such a good time that it became one of my favorite cities in the world. The Messengers played at the Jazz Workshop on Boylston. During the day, Art and I walked around arm in arm soaking up history, laughing and smiling at anything even slightly amusing, and stuffing ourselves on seafood. I was falling in love all over again.

Shortly after we got back to Atlantic City, Art opened a checking account and signed a power of attorney form giving me authority over it. He had bookshelves and elegant white wicker furniture delivered to the apartment Jane and I shared and gave me money to buy us a beautiful, only slightly used, beige, Cadillac (driven only on Sunday by a preacher), and a used Ford station wagon we named Big Green.

He must have known I'd soon find us a house with room for bookshelves, wicker and more. And yes, a two-car garage. The white stucco house on Mill Road in Northfield was a unique blend of English and Spanish architecture, a big friendly house with green shutters, a red roof, and grounds covering a whole square block. There was even a summerhouse out back which we filled with the white wicker. Mischievous poltergeists inhabited the basement, where they kept rearranging everything but the washer and dryer. I guess the appliances were too heavy.

Some local old-timers said the ghost of Evelyn Nesbit, the girl in the red velvet swing, roamed the third floor. One version of the story is that Evelyn was a showgirl at the Silver Slipper Supper Club in Atlantic City, where men sipped champagne from her slippers in the 1920s. She was married to millionaire Harry Thaw, but the love of her life was the famous architect Stanford White. In a jealous rage, Thaw shot and killed White at Madison Square Garden. Before his untimely demise, White had built an indoor swing with red cords coming down from the ceiling and a red velvet seat for Evelyn's amusement in their romantic Northfield getaway. After the scandal of the shooting, Evelyn was forever known as the "Girl in the Red Velvet Swing."

Others insisted Evelyn never lived there but the former mayor of Longport, a seaside community a few miles away, once inhabited the place. Personally, I love the legend about our magnificent home being built for the beautiful Evelyn, even though in reality she probably did her swinging in the cottage on Steelman Avenue across the street.

Just before Labor Day, 1976, Takashi came to live with us. A few days afterwards he entered first grade at Mount Vernon Avenue School. Atsuko, still sickly, had not sent him to either the preschool or kindergarten in which I had enrolled him. But she didn't object when Art threw Takashi's things into Big Green and the three of us headed to New Jersey. I've always felt she didn't make a fuss because she loved her son and wanted the best for him.

She still would be able to talk to him on the phone as often as she wished and we would bring him into the city for weekends and vacations whenever she wanted.

As for my feelings, I was overjoyed. No more being just a part-time family. Now we were whole.

Drawing by Kathleen M. Arleth

Our home, our spiritual haven.

Photo by Lou Jones

Art at Lou's Boston studio while in town for a
gig at the Jazz Workshop.

August 24, 1962 Photo copyright Raymond Ross archives/CTSImages.com

Art conducting in the dressing room.

Photo by Bertil Mollberger

In Bertil's own words, this is a picture of "Mr. Blakey at nightclub Wictoria in Gävle, Sweden, 6th of March, 1981."

Photo by Gunnar Holmberg

Art (center), Bobby Watson (left) and Dennis Irwin (right)
getting festive in Sweden.

The Fine Art of Cookin' and Jammin'

I play my sonatas on the stove.

Nella Rubenstein, wife of pianist
and composer Anton Rubenstein

The yellow-tiled kitchen was the heart of our home life. It was where we three thrived on making up new recipes and trying them out on each other.

We thought of it as a piece of New Orleans transported to New Jersey because it always was filled with a gumbo of spicy music and enticing aromas that brought a smile to everybody's face. No one ever used our front door. Everybody came in the back door and plopped down in the kitchen.

It was easy to see why New Orleans foods appealed to Art so much. Everything is just the right mix of classical French, Spanish, German, Indian, African, Southern soul, improvisation, fresh locally grown ingredients, and unbridled passion. Pow!

I began to realize that cooking is an art form, revealing as much about us as the pictures we paint or the songs we write. The good ones nourish our minds and spirits, penetrating our souls with their flavor; sometimes bittersweet, other times salty or savory.

The recipes that follow tell Art's story just as surely as a narrative. Like sheet music, recipes are jumping off points for improvisation. No food writer can tell you how many carrots you like in your beef stew or how hot you want your chili. In everything you cook, you give a part of your unique self.

While you're mixing and chopping, if you're old school, put on your vinyl "A Night in Tunesia" with the volume way up. If you're new school, pull out your MP3. Now you're cookin' and jammin' in the incomparable University of Blakey!

The ability to follow a recipe, we decided, was irrelevant... Most good cooks never do. They judge things by sights, tastes, and smell, adding a splash of this and a pinch of that – artists building up their canvas. Recipes should be only rough guides (with the exception of baking) and to follow one exactly is a bit like painting by numbers.

Sallyann J. Murphy, The Zen of Food

Photo by Cairati

One of many photos lovingly taken of Art in Italy by his friend, Enea Cairati.

Road Food

When we offer this gift [food] to the person we love, we are not only nourishing each other's bodies, we are feeding one another's spirit.

Daphne Rose Kingma, Author

Before we graduated to the four-burner gas range on Mill Road or even the two-burner hot plate at the Roger Williams, we cooked on the road.

In the 1970s and 80s, most hotel and motel rooms didn't even have a mini-fridge, let alone a microwave or a stove. If we were lucky, there'd be a greasy hot plate, an iron skillet, and a sauce pot. That was all we needed. We'd stock up at the nearest supermarket or neighborhood mom-and-pop store and start cookin'.

Skillet Chili – *About 4 generous servings*

The first meal I made for Art was an old black iron skillet of chili. I simmered it on a one-burner hot plate in a tired Woodward Avenue motel, and we ate it with Ritz crackers. It was a good day for chili. February in Detroit has 28 good days for chili. Art was all smiles sitting there on the edge of that lumpy bed. It made me realize how much he and lots of other musicians on the road hunger for the familiar tastes and smells of home.

¾ pound, more or less, lean ground beef (I use chuck, round or
   sirloin.)
Salt, pepper, paprika, and garlic powder to taste
1 green pepper, coarsely chopped
1 stalk celery, chopped
1 medium onion, coarsely chopped
2 15½ -ounce cans red kidney beans
2 tablespoons chili powder or an amount to taste
1 28-ounce can crushed tomatoes with added puree
2 tablespoons sugar

Season beef with salt, pepper, paprika, and garlic powder. In skillet over medium-high heat, brown beef with green pepper, celery, and onion. Stir to break up the meat. If there is any grease left in the pan after the meat is browned, drain it off. Combine chili powder with the beans and add to skillet. Combine tomatoes and sugar. Add to skillet. Simmer over low heat 30 minutes. Check for seasonings.

Jazz it up: Serve it over rice and top it with sour cream, chopped scallions, shredded cheese, shredded cabbage, chopped tomatoes, and chopped fresh cilantro.

COOK'S NOTES IMPROVISATIONS & VARIATIONS

Beefy Crockery Chili – *About 6 to 8 servings*

At home, with more ingredients at hand, we had fun experimenting and came up with the following fancy crockery pot version.

8 bacon strips, cut into bite-size pieces
2 pounds, more or less, beef stew meat, cut into bite-size pieces
Salt, pepper, and garlic powder to taste
1 28-ounce can peeled tomatoes in tomato juice, broken up
1 14½ -ounce can peeled tomatoes in tomato juice broken up
1 16-ounce can tomato sauce
2 to 3 heaping tablespoons brown or white sugar or to taste
2 15½ -ounce cans red kidney beans, rinsed and drained
3 tablespoons chili powder or an amount to taste
2 cups baby carrots, thinly sliced and salted to taste
1 medium to large onion, coarsely chopped
1 cup celery, chopped
1 green pepper, coarsely chopped
¼ cup fresh parsley, minced
1 teaspoon ground cumin

Cook bacon in skillet over medium heat just until crisp. Drain on paper towel. Brown beef in bacon drippings. Add salt, pepper, garlic powder, and sugar and add to pot. Combine beans and chili powder and add to pot. Add remaining ingredients and stir well. Cover, cook on low for 6 to 8 hours or until meat is tender. Taste and adjust seasonings if needed.

Note: This deserves a loaf of the best French or Italian bread you can find. A green salad with your favorite vinaigrette dressing goes well, too. Make a second meal by serving what's left over spaghetti.

Turn this into chicken chili by browning a chicken breast cut into bite-size pieces in the bacon drippings instead of using beef.

COOK'S NOTES IMPROVISATIONS & VARIATIONS

Crockery Veggie Chili – *About 4 servings*

1 cup baby carrots, thinly sliced and salted
1 cup drained canned corn or fresh or frozen
  corn, salted and
  peppered to taste
1 cup fresh zucchini, chopped
21 -ounces undrained tomatoes, broken up,
  plus 2 heaping tablespoons
  brown or white sugar
Garlic powder to taste
1 8-ounce can tomato sauce plus 1 teaspoon
  brown or white sugar

1 medium or large onion, coarsely chopped
1 cup celery, chopped
½ green pepper, coarsely chopped
¼ cup fresh parsley, minced (I like Italian
  parsley.)
1 15-ounce can red kidney beans, rinsed and
  drained
1 heaping tablespoon chili powder
½ teaspoon ground cumin
1 cup fresh cilantro, chopped
1 teaspoon kosher salt
1 teaspoon hot pepper sauce
1 15-ounce can (or smaller if you prefer)
  chickpeas, rinsed, drained, salted and garlic
  powder to taste

*Put carrots, corn, and zucchini in crockery pot.
Combine sugared tomatoes and garlic powder;
add to pot. Add sugared tomato sauce. Add
onion, celery, green pepper, and parsley to pot.
Combine beans and chili powder and add to pot.
Add cilantro, cumin, salt, and hot pepper sauce.
Mix well. Cover and cook on low for 5 to 6 hours.
Add chickpeas last 5 minutes. Taste and adjust
seasonings if needed.*

Serve this with a pan of warm cornbread.

COOK'S NOTES IMPROVISATIONS & VARIATIONS

Borscht

In all our years of travel, one of the meals we savored the most was in a Montreal apartment hotel. It was lovingly prepared by Messengers trumpeter Valery Ponomarev and his wife, Tanjana. A simple meal of borscht, bread, and fruit prepared just as they had made it in Russia before moving to the States.

Art had been to Russia and eaten borscht many times. This was my first taste and I loved it. We immediately agreed to add it to our soup repertoire. As I ate the borscht, I wondered why this soup had never caught on in my hometown. Everybody there had a garden where they grew the necessary veggies, including the all-important beets.

What we enjoyed so much about the meal wasn't just the taste of the food. It was that two people we cared about took time to share something so special with us.

At home, we made a crockery pot version. Here it is:

Follow the recipe for vegetable beef soup on page 112. Add a cup of thinly sliced cabbage and a cup of drained canned or fresh cooked beets, diced, the last half hour of cooking. Top each bowl with a dollop of sour cream just before serving.
Serve with good fresh brown bread.

COOK'S NOTES

IMPROVISATIONS & VARIATIONS

Sunday Dinner

Sunday dinner is Sunday dinner no matter where you are. Two of our stand-bys were smothered chicken and jambalaya served with rice and a simple green salad. Art chopped and peeled. I stirred. Dessert was whatever fresh fruit was in season.

Smothered Chicken
– 2 to 3 generous servings

2 pounds chicken thighs (4 to 6 thighs)
Salt, freshly ground black pepper, and garlic
   powder to taste
Flour
2 tablespoons olive oil
1 large onion, coarsely chopped
1 green bell pepper, coarsely chopped
½ cup fresh Italian parsley, chopped
1 cup white wine

Rinse and pat dry chicken. Season with salt, pepper, and garlic powder. Heat the oil in a deep frying pan. Flour the chicken. Brown the chicken over medium-high heat. Remove chicken to paper towels. In the same pan, sauté onion over medium-high heat until tender. Add green pepper and parsley the last minute. Add wine.

Add chicken and spoon the veggies over it. Adjust the heat to medium-low, cover and cook 1-1/2 to 2 hours until the chicken is tender (almost falling off the bone). Add more wine during cooking if needed.

New Orleans/Jersey Jambalaya – *4 servings*

Olive oil
¼ pound hot Italian sausage
1 medium onion, coarsely chopped
1 green pepper, coarsely chopped
3 cloves garlic, coarsely chopped
¾ pound medium cooked shrimp, peeled, deveined, salted, peppered, and garlic powdered
1 14½-ounce can stewed tomatoes
2-ounces tomato juice
1 heaping tablespoon sugar
½ teaspoon thyme
½ teaspoon oregano

Heat oil in skillet. Add sausage. Cook over medium-high heat until browned. Stir to break up meat as it cooks. Drain on paper towel. Wipe out skillet; add more oil. When the oil is hot, add the onion. Sauté it, stirring often, 3 minutes. Add green bell pepper and sauté 2 to 3 minutes longer. Add garlic and shrimp. Sauté over medium heat just until the shrimp are hot. Combine the tomatoes, tomato juice, and sugar. Add to pan and cook over medium heat until tomatoes are heated through. Stir in thyme and oregano.

This is terrific served over any rice, but brown rice is especially good.

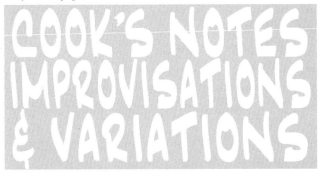

Spring and Summer Salads

In the spring and summer, or even in the winter if we were in California or Florida, we ate lots of fresh produce, sometimes in salads, but often just rinsed and eaten out of hand. Art, who never slept much, would get up and go out to the green market or a farm stand and bring back fruits and vegetables that had been picked that morning. One of his favorite stops was the Reading Terminal Market in Philadelphia. If there was a park nearby, we'd grab a blanket and pack a paper bag picnic.

Art's Summer Salad

Art wasn't one to write down amounts for recipes. He liked to improvise too much for that. As with all recipes, use amounts that please you, just as he did.

Macaroni
Cooked chicken, diced
Grated carrots
Fresh tomato chunks
Mayonnaise or bottled dressing
Salt and pepper

Combine and refrigerate.

Art's Tomato Salad

Fresh tomatoes, cut into chunks
Fresh Italian parsley, finely chopped
Red onion, sliced
Vinaigrette dressing (3 parts extra-virgin olive oil to 1 part vinegar)
Salt and pepper
Sliced deli baked ham, chopped

Toss the veggies with dressing. Salt and pepper to taste. Top with ham.

Note: When he came back with good cheese, he added that to the mix, too.

Art's Spinach Salad

Fresh spinach
Red onion or scallions, sliced
Fresh mushrooms, sliced
Grated carrots
Vinaigrette or dressing of your choice
Salt and pepper

Toss and enjoy

Note: This basic salad sometimes also contained sliced radishes, raisins, fresh tomatoes (chunks or whole cherry tomatoes), cashews, pine nuts or walnuts.

Art's N'Awlinz Shrimp Salad
– 4 servings

Knowing how much I love shrimp every which way, Art made this shrimp salad for me. As you see, the recipe makes 4 portions – one for Art, three for me. Someone in the French Market told him a general recipe, then, of course, he improvised. I hope you'll do the same.

¾ cup, more or less, mayonnaise to which you've added mustard to taste

A bunch of green onions, chopped (If you grew up in the South or Midwest, you probably still call them green onions. If you grew up in the East, you know them as scallions. I've heard both words in the West.)

2 stalks celery, finely chopped

1 or 2 drops Louisiana hot sauce

2 pounds shrimp, cooked and peeled

Lemon wedges

Combine everything but the shrimp and lemon. Pour over shrimp and stir. Refrigerate until ready to serve with lemon slices for garnish.

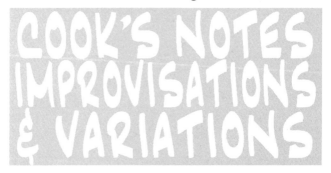

COOK'S NOTES IMPROVISATIONS & VARIATIONS

Jessie's Gulf Coast Crab and Tomato Salad – *4 servings*

This recipe and the following one for shrimp salad came to me from the Gulf by way of Princeton, New Jersey.

1 pound fresh crabmeat
3 tablespoons mayonnaise
2 tablespoons salad oil (I substitute good extra-virgin olive oil.)
1 tablespoon vinegar
½ teaspoon sugar
Salt and pepper to taste (I add pepper, no salt.)
4 fresh from the field or garden tomatoes
Crisp lettuce

Mix the crab with mayonnaise, oil, vinegar, and seasonings. Try not to break up the crabmeat while you're doing this. Refrigerate until ready to serve. Hollow out the tomatoes and fill them with the crab mixture. Arrange on lettuce leaves.

Jessie's Gulf Coast Shrimp Salad

– 4 servings

1 teaspoon salad oil (I substitute good quality extra-virgin olive oil.)
3 tablespoons catsup
Salt and pepper to taste (I add pepper, no salt.)
2 tablespoons mayonnaise
1 teaspoon vinegar
2 tablespoons green pepper, finely chopped
½ teaspoon sugar
Dash of celery seed (On the road, I didn't go out and buy celery seed, but I did use it at home.)
1 pound fresh shrimp cooked and peeled
Crisp lettuce
4 fresh tomatoes, quartered

Make the sauce by mixing everything but the shrimp, tomatoes and lettuce. Add the shrimp and mix again. Refrigerate until ready to serve in the quartered tomatoes over lettuce.

COOK'S NOTES IMPROVISATIONS & VARIATIONS

Chops

Come autumn, Art had a knack for finding the best butcher stalls in the farmers markets and the small neighborhood meat markets where everything was cut to order. What joy! He'd bring back bone-in pork chops of just the right thickness, about ¾ inch. No resemblance to the puny boneless things at the supermarket.

Smothered Pork Chops – *2 servings*

2 ¾-inch thick pork chops
Salt, pepper, garlic powder to taste
All-purpose flour
Olive oil
Sliced onion
⅓ cup white wine
1 10½ -ounce can or jar pork gravy

Sprinkle chops with seasonings. Heat oil in saute' pan over medium heat. Flour chops. Add chops to pan. Brown for 6 minutes, turn, and brown for 3 additional minutes. Turn heat to low. Top chops with sliced onion. Add wine to pan. Cover. Simmer 20 minutes. Add about ¾ of the can of gravy. Simmer 10 minutes. Add the remaining gravy and simmer 10 minutes more.

COOK'S NOTES
IMPROVISATIONS
& VARIATIONS

Creole Pork Chops – *2 servings*

2 medium bone-in pork chops
Salt, pepper, garlic powder, and paprika to taste
Olive Oil
1 medium onion sliced
¼ cup celery, chopped
¼ cup green pepper, diced
1 14½ -ounce can stewed tomatoes
¼ cup red wine

*Sprinkle chops with salt, pepper, garlic powder,
and paprika. Brown well in oil over medium-high
heat. Place onion slices over chops. Turn heat
down to low. In a bowl, mix celery, green pepper,
tomatoes, and wine. Pour over chops. Cover.
Simmer 45 minutes or until chops are tender.
Cooking time will depend on how thick the chops
are.*

COOK'S NOTES
IMPROVISATIONS
& VARIATIONS

Home Cooking

You don't have to cook fancy or complicated masterpieces – just good food from fresh ingredients.

Julia Child, Chef, Cookbook Author, TV Personality

Like all families, Art, Takashi, and I had rituals. Art's homecomings went like this. First bear hugs all around. His arms were short, but Art's upper body strength from all those years behind the drums was enormous. Overlapping the take-your-breath-away hugs were the ear-to-ear grins and an assortment of sloppy kisses. I remember laughing, crying, and trying to talk, all at the same time.

There was the unlocking of the huge light-brown soft leather suitcase which held the many presents that Art hadn't already sent us by mail. And what gifts they were. When he was seven, Takashi got authentic gray suede Tyrolean short pants which I loved and forced him to wear to our friends Marjorie and Paul's wedding. I haven't checked with him lately to see if he's forgiven me yet. Takashi's favorites were all things Swiss, including a prized army knife and a host of assorted chocolates. I was showered with everything from blue silk sheets to a dainty gold German antique watch.

Gift giving would be followed by profuse thank-yous and a second round of hugs, and kisses, and grins.

Simultaneously, the family pets would perform their "Art's home" dance. Libra, our gentle large mixed-breed dog who suffered from arthritis, would wag her tail and look up at Art with those deep brown eyes. He'd kneel down to pet her and she'd put her beautiful tan face against his and lick his cheeks and nose. Pasha, our assertive curly black toy poodle, wasted no time climbing right up into Art's arms for her turn at kissing. Pasha knew about the road first hand. She often jumped into her vented beige shoulder bag and accompanied us on tour. Her road credits included Carnegie Hall, the Louvre, and the Montreux Jazz Festival. The youngest member of the pet family was Baby Noel, a black-and-tan Yorkie who started life as the runt of the litter but soon grew to tower over his biological siblings. I named him in honor of a handsome French boy we met in Paris some years before. Baby Noel would follow Pasha's lead and leap into Art's arms.

Lastly came Charlemagne ("Charmer"), a grand Persian lilac cat rescued in his infancy from the roadside where he'd been tossed and abandoned. "Charmer" would majestically take his place snuggled against Art's belly, purring contentedly as he was stroked. Finally, Art would head for the upstairs shower to wash off the road and ease into the sweet taste and feel of home at the Jersey shore.

He treasured his time between gigs. Nobody appreciated shore life more than he did. Everything refreshed him – the grapes from our own arbor; the flounder and blues caught off the coast; the salt air against his weathered face as we walked the Ocean City boardwalk; and the farms with their fields of tender yellow sweet corn, juicy Big Boy tomatoes, tiny early peas, and U-pick apple orchards.

Art's favorite supper was fish any-which-way, peas, and applesauce. Not a hard man to please, especially when you consider he did the shopping, peeled the apples, and shelled the peas. Art was a regular at Tull's fish market. He knew what time daily the fresh seafood would arrive, and he would make sure he was there to meet the delivery. He took his food shopping seriously. When it came to procuring produce, he eliminated the middleman and went straight to the farm.

And so the house on Mill Road, which always was full of fragrant flowers, including roses from our own yard, also brimmed with the scents of citrus, strawberries, and tomatoes. The only fresh fruits Art had tasted growing up were an occasional soft brown banana, a sour green apple he found on the ground, and on rare Christmases, a tangerine.

He had no recollection of ever having had a fresh vegetable, and remembered the tuna and salmon he ate came from a dented can. Flowers were something seen only at funerals, usually white carnations placed near the casket by sobbing old ladies in black. No wonder he surrounded himself and those he loved with all that was fresh.

Many a morning during the South Jersey growing season, from April asparagus through November cranberries, he'd spend his time on the back roads going from farm stand to farm stand in search of the best produce.

He reveled in swapping stories with farm hands, families, or whoever else took time to sit on the farmhouse porch with him. And usually he even managed to talk the farmer into letting him venture into the fields to pick his own. He'd come home with a trunk full of grand tastes – plump Jersey tomatoes piled oh so carefully into a tall basket, a brown paper bag bulging with sweet white corn on the cob, yellow-red-orange peaches almost bursting with juices laid gently side-by-side in a crate so as not to bruise them.

And' oh yes, he'd have a head full of stories to tell, too. I think if Art hadn't been the greatest jazz drummer ever to grace this planet, he could have been a damn good farmer.

Summer Flounder Baked in Herbs and Wine – *4 servings*

Flounder was the fish we ate most often, so mild, agreeable, and easy to prepare.

Cooking spray
2 pounds summer flounder fillets, rinsed and
   patted dry with a paper towel
3 tablespoons butter, melted
3 tablespoons extra-virgin olive oil
2 tablespoons fresh lemon juice
1/3 cup white wine
1 teaspoon fresh basil, minced
1/2 cup fresh parsley, chopped
1/2 cup scallions, sliced

Preheat oven to 375 degrees.

Arrange fillets in a lightly sprayed shallow baking dish. Combine remaining ingredients and pour over fish. Bake 20 minutes or until fish flakes easily when pierced with a knife or fork.

Serve with a bottle of Louisiana hot sauce on the table.

Art's Sautéed Summer Flounder with Fine Herbs

Summer flounder fillets, rinsed and patted dry
  with paper towel
Butter
Milk
All-purpose flour
Fresh parsley, chives, tarragon, and chervil which
  have been rinsed, patted dry, and minced
Lemon wedges

Heat sauté pan and melt a generous amount of butter in it. Dip the fillets in milk and roll them gently in flour. Shake off excess flour. Brown over medium-high heat, turn and brown on the other side. Browning can take as little as a minute or two depending on the thickness of the fillets. The fillets are done when they flake easily at the thickest part as they are pierced with a knife or fork. Remove them to a hot platter which you have warmed in a 200 degree oven.

Melt a little more butter in the pan and add equal amounts of parsley, chives, tarragon, and chervil. A general guide is to use about 1 teaspoon of each herb to every 4 tablespoons of melted butter. Again, I emphasize adding amounts that are pleasing to you. Heat and stir gently for only a few seconds and pour over the fish.

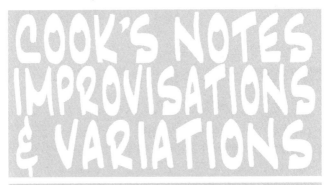

Sautéed Flounder with Lemon Butter Sauce - *2 generous servings*

About 2 tablespoons butter plus more as needed
1 pound flounder fillets, rinsed and patted dry with a paper towel
Kosher salt and freshly ground pepper to taste
2 tablespoons chopped parsley leaves
1 teaspoon chopped garlic
1 tablespoon fresh lemon juice
Lemon slices

Melt butter in a large saute' pan over medium heat. Turn the heat up to medium-high. Saute' salted and peppered fillets until just lightly browned. Depending on the thickness of the fillets, this will take 1 or 2 minutes. Turn the fish and cook for 1 minute. Check for doneness. The fish is done when it turns opaque and flakes easily at the thickest part when a knife or fork is inserted.

Remove the fish to warm platters.

Turn the heat down to medium. Add more butter to the pan so that total melted butter is about 3 tablespoons. Add the parsley, garlic, and lemon juice. Saute' for 2 minutes. Spoon some sauce over the fillets on each platter. Garnish with lemon slices. Serve immediately.

Don't forget to have a bottle of Louisiana hot sauce on the table.

COOK'S NOTES IMPROVISATIONS & VARIATIONS

Flounder on a Tomato Bed - *2 servings*

2 medium fresh tomatoes, thinly sliced
Kosher salt
Freshly ground pepper
Seasoned Italian breadcrumbs
1 pound flounder fillets, rinsed and patted dry
  with a paper towel (about 6 thin fillets)
½ cup white wine

4 tablespoons butter
1 teaspoon lemon juice
Freshly grated Parmesan cheese
Paprika
1 lemon, cut into wedges

Preheat oven to 500 degrees.

Butter a baking pan or dish large enough to hold the fillets in a single layer. Salt and pepper the tomatoes and lay slices side by side in the pan. Top tomatoes with a light covering of breadcrumbs. Arrange fillets over the tomatoes. Lightly salt and pepper them.

Meanwhile, combine wine, butter, and lemon juice in a small saucepan. Bring to a boil over medium heat and cook 2 minutes. Pour over fish. Sprinkle fish with cheese and squeeze of lemon. Bake 8 minutes or until fillets turn opaque and flake when a knife or fork is inserted. Thin fillets will be done to perfection in 8 minutes. Sprinkle with paprika. Serve with lemon wedges.

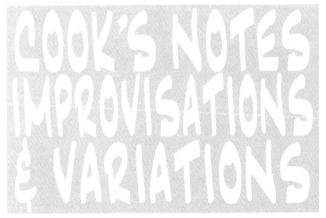

COOK'S NOTES IMPROVISATIONS & VARIATIONS

Sautéed Flounder in a Flash – *2 servings*

1 pound flounder fillets, rinsed and thoroughly
   dried
½ teaspoon red pepper (cayenne)
½ teaspoon freshly ground black pepper
Kosher salt
Flour
About 2 tablespoons or less butter melted in a
   non-stick sauté pan
Chopped parsley
1 lemon or lime, quartered

*Salt and pepper fillets. Dredge lightly in flour.
Sauté over medium-high heat a minute or two on
each side. Thin fillets will be done in a minute per
side. They will turn opaque and flake when tested
with a knife or fork. Garnish with parsley and
lemon or lime wedges. Serve immediately, and
pass the Louisiana hot sauce around the table.*

Note: Keep your flounder comfortable. If all the
fillets won't fit side by side in the pan, don't crowd
them; just use two pans.

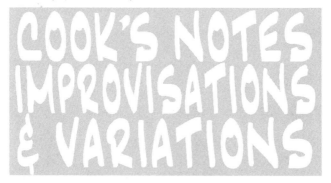

Broiled Bluefish

Preheat the broiler.

Measure the thickness of the fish. Ideally, they will be three-quarters to 1 inch thick. Pat them dry with a paper towel. Lay them on a greased broiler pan and baste with melted butter or lightly coat with oil. Baste again after 4 or 5 minutes. Allow 8 to 10 minutes of cooking time per inch. They will flake when touched with a fork to signal they are done. Add a generous squeeze of fresh lemon, kosher salt, and freshly ground pepper to taste, and serve with a bottle of Louisiana hot sauce.

Variation: Spread light mayonnaise instead of butter or oil over the fillets or steaks. Sprinkle with freshly grated Parmesan cheese and broil as directed.

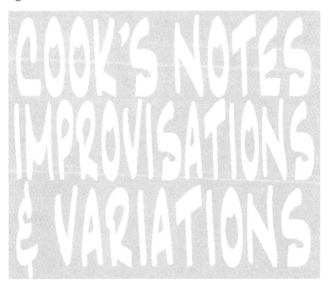

Myra's Marinated Blues – *4 servings*

2 pounds bluefish steaks
2 tablespoons light soy sauce
2 tablespoons wine vinegar
2 tablespoons fresh lemon juice
2 tablespoons oil
2 tablespoons fresh chopped parsley
1 teaspoon minced garlic
½ teaspoon freshly ground black pepper
Lemon slices

Measure the thickness of the steaks. Place steaks in glass dish. Combine next 7 ingredients and pour over the fish. Marinate in fridge for 1 hour. Remove steaks. Discard marinade.

Preheat the broiler. Grease the broiler pan and follow broiling instructions in the above recipe for broiled bluefish. Serve with lemon slices.

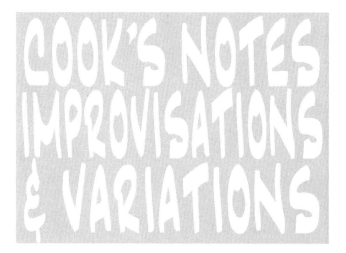

COOK'S NOTES IMPROVISATIONS & VARIATIONS

Sautéed Tuna – *4 servings*

Olive oil
4 tuna steaks, rinsed and patted dry
Freshly ground black pepper to taste
Lemon wedges

Coat the bottom of a large skillet with oil. Preheat the pan for a couple of minutes. Add peppered tuna. Cook over medium to medium-high heat for about 4 minutes on each side. Remove fish as soon as it flakes with a fork. Serve with your favorite salsa or butter sauce and lemon wedges.

Note: Easy Butter Sauce: To each half-pound of melted butter, add 1 or 2 cloves of garlic, chopped and gently simmered for a minute or so with 1 tablespoon minced fresh parsley.

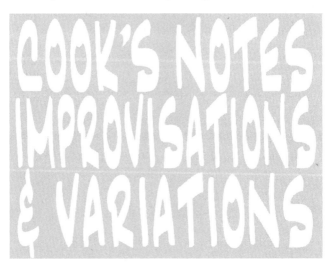

COOK'S NOTES IMPROVISATIONS & VARIATIONS

Grilled Tuna with Cucumber Sauce

Art loved to cook on a little no-frills grill he picked up at the hardware store.

The Tuna:

Rinse and pat dry 1-inch-thick steaks and brush them with olive oil. Coat the grill rack with oil or nonstick cooking spray. When the charcoal is medium hot, lay the steaks on the grill. For medium well, grill about 5 minutes a side. Baste with more oil when you turn the steaks. Well-done will take a little longer and rare will take only half the time. To signal that it's done, the meat will flake when you insert a fork or sharp knife. Nobody can tell you exactly how long to grill tuna. You'll be the best judge of that. My only caution is not to overcook it because it'll get dry and tough. Salt and pepper fish to taste.

The Sauce: About 2½ cups

1 medium cucumber, rinsed, peeled, seeded,
   and chopped
Kosher salt to taste
¾ cup reduced-fat sour cream
¼ cup light mayonnaise
1 clove garlic, minced
1 heaping tablespoon chopped scallions
2 teaspoons fresh lime or lemon juice
Freshly ground black pepper to taste
2 tablespoons of one of the following:
Snipped fresh dill
Chopped fresh parsley

Torn fresh basil
Chopped fresh cilantro

Place the chopped cucumber in a colander and sprinkle with a dash of salt. Leave the colander in the sink for 15 minutes. Pat the cucumber pieces dry with a paper towel. Meanwhile combine the sour cream, mayonnaise, garlic, scallions, and juice. Mix in the cucumber pieces. Add pepper to taste. Stir in one of the herbs. Refrigerate covered 1 hour. Stir before serving with tuna.

Note: Try this sauce with salmon, too.

Grilled Tuna with Tomato Topper
– 4 servings

The Tomatoes:

4 small tomatoes, rinsed, quartered, salted, and peppered
1 teaspoon or more to taste of one of the following:
　Chopped fresh oregano
　Chopped fresh parsley
　Torn fresh basil
　Chopped cilantro
　Thinly sliced scallions

¼ cup extra-virgin olive oil
1 clove garlic, minced

Combine all ingredients and allow to sit at room temperature while you prepare the grilled tuna.

The Tuna:

Follow the directions previously given for grilling tuna. Cook one steak per person. Plate the tuna and top it with the tomato mixture.

COOK'S NOTES IMPROVISATIONS & VARIATIONS

Grilled Cape May Scallops – *6 servings*

½ cup light soy sauce
1 tablespoon sugar
2 teaspoons fresh lemon juice
1 teaspoon sesame oil
1 clove garlic, minced
2 tablespoons white wine
3 pounds sea scallops, gently rinsed and
  thoroughly dried
Lemon or lime wedges for garnish

Mix first 6 ingredients in a large bowl. Add scallops. Cover the bowl and refrigerate for one hour. Thread the scallops on skewers. If you use wooden or bamboo skewers, don't forget to soak them in cold water for 30 minutes before grilling. Spray the grill rack with cooking spray.

*Grill over medium-hot charcoal until scallops turn
opaque all the way through. Turn and brush with
marinade as needed during grilling. For testing
doneness, pierce one with a knife. The main thing
to remember is not to overcook them. They can
quickly go from succulent to rubbery. Serve with
lemon or lime wedges and have some Louisiana
hot sauce on the table.*

COOK'S NOTES
IMPROVISATIONS
& VARIATIONS

Sautéed Scallops with Tomatoes
– 3 servings

1½ pounds sea scallops, gently rinsed,
   thoroughly dried and cut into quarters
Flour
3 tablespoons butter and 3 tablespoons
   vegetable or extra-virgin olive oil
3 cloves garlic, minced
Kosher salt and freshly ground black pepper to
   taste
1 large tomato, rinsed and cut into chunks
⅓ cup, more or less to taste, finely chopped
   parsley
Lemon wedges

*Flour scallops and shake off any excess flour. Heat
a large skillet or saute' pan over medium-high
heat for two minutes. Add butter and oil. When*

*butter has melted, add scallops and cook about
three minutes, turning scallops as needed to coat
them with the butter and oil and brown them.
Add garlic, salt, and pepper. Add tomato chunks
and cook only until tomatoes are hot and scallops
are done. Be sure not to overcook this dish
because scallops will toughen. They are finished
when they are opaque all the way through. To
check for doneness, pierce one with a knife or cut
one in half. The exact cooking time depends on
the thickness of the scallops. Add parsley. Serve
with lemon wedges.*

Note: Don't crowd scallops. Use two pans if
necessary

Asparagus

Two early signs of spring at our house were the beautiful yellow forsythia blooming in every direction and Art walking in with an armful of fresh tender asparagus.

Blanched Asparagus

When given a choice, I gravitate toward the easiest way of doing things. In this case, I go with blanching just until the spears are tender-crisp. For very thin spears, the time can be as short as two minutes. To prep the asparagus for blanching, snap the stalks where they break off naturally and rinse under cold running water. Lay the spears in a large pan, cover them with boiling water, and set the heat on medium. Check for doneness with a sharp knife. When they are just right, drain them immediately and wipe them with a paper towel. Nobody likes soggy spears. Sprinkle with kosher salt.

Improvise:

Add a dash of soy sauce, a splash of fresh lime or lemon juice, or a finely chopped scallion to melted butter and pour over the asparagus.

Add fresh lemon or lime juice to a dollop of mayonnaise. Serve the mayo cold and the asparagus at room temperature.

Drizzle asparagus ever so lightly with your favorite vinaigrette and serve at room temperature.

Drizzle asparagus with almond butter. Melt two tablespoons butter in a small pan over low heat. Add a tablespoon of sliced almonds. Heat and stir almonds for a minute and spoon over asparagus.

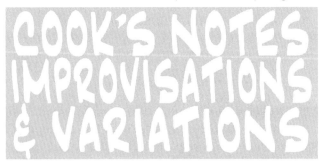

COOK'S NOTES IMPROVISATIONS & VARIATIONS

Garlic Asparagus – *4 servings*

2 pounds asparagus, blanched and drained
3 tablespoons extra-virgin olive oil
6 cloves garlic, peeled and thinly sliced
1 lemon, sliced
Salt and freshly ground black pepper to taste

Arrange blanched asparagus on a platter. Heat oil
in small skillet over medium heat. Add garlic and
sauté one minute. Pour over asparagus. Season
with salt and freshly ground pepper. Drizzle
with the juice of two lemon slices. Garnish with
remaining lemon slices.

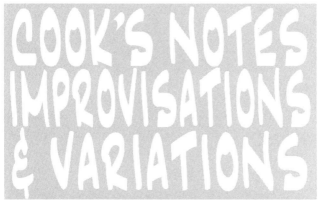

Sesame Asparagus – *2 generous servings*

1 pound blanched and drained asparagus
  spears, salted to taste
3 tablespoons butter
1½ tablespoons fresh lemon juice
1 ½ teaspoons sesame seeds

In a small pan, combine butter, lemon juice, and sesame seeds. Cook over low heat, stirring occasionally, until butter is melted and seeds are golden. Spoon the sesame butter over the asparagus.

Note: Turn this into a one-dish meal by combining it with a pound of peeled, cleaned, deveined shrimp you've sautéed in butter or olive oil, and placing it over a bed of yellow rice.

Strawberries

The first fruit of the season in New Jersey is strawberries. Art would come home with quarts of them which he had picked himself in a local farmer's patch. We'd wash some and eat them out of hand right away.

Glazed Strawberries

Sometimes the three of us – Art, Takashi, and I – collaborated on making glazed strawberries. About an hour before dinner, Art would rinse the berries, pat them dry with a paper towel, and leave them out on the counter. Room temperature brings out their flavor.

Hint: Don't wash berries until you're ready to use them because washed ones decay quickly.

I'd make the glaze by melting some strawberry jelly (not jam or preserves) in a small pan over medium heat, stirring occasionally. I'd pour it into a bowl and set it on the counter to cool a bit. Meantime, Art would cut the tops off most of the berries, saving some with leaves on for a pretty garnish. Then it was Takashi's turn to pour the glaze over all the berries. Immediately we'd all reach for some right off the counter. As for the rest, here are a few things we did with them.

Spooned them into clear glass bowls or goblets and topped them with freshly whipped cream and mint sprigs.

Filled baked puff pastry shells with berries. (I used Pepperidge Farm frozen shells.) Serve with whipped cream on the side.

Topped an angel food cake with berries, putting the pointy ends up. Fill the center with whipped cream if you wish. Garnish with whole berries.

Note: Add the whipped cream to these desserts at the last moment for the best presentation and taste.

COOK'S NOTES IMPROVISATIONS & VARIATIONS

Strawberry Ice Cream Pie – *4 servings*

1 cup milk
1 pint strawberry ice cream
1 3.4-ounce package strawberry or vanilla
   instant pudding mix
1 9-inch graham cracker crust
1 pint fresh rinsed strawberries
Whipped cream

*Combine milk and ice cream in mixing bowl.
Blend until smooth. Add pudding mix and stir
until well mixed, about one minute. Pour into
crust. Cover with plastic wrap. Put in freezer to set.
Leave in freezer two hours or until ready to serve.
Garnish with fresh strawberries and whipped
cream just before serving.*

COOK'S NOTES
IMPROVISATIONS
& VARIATIONS

Art's Bourbon Berries

Fresh whole strawberries
Bourbon
Confectioners, white, or brown sugar
Whipped cream or sour cream

*Rinse and pat dry the berries with a paper towel.
Get out the bourbon and pour some into a bowl.*

Put a little sugar in a separate bowl. Put a lot of whipped cream or sour cream in another bowl. Dunk a berry in the bourbon, then sugar, and finally into the whipped cream. Eat it out of hand.

COOK'S NOTES IMPROVISATIONS & VARIATIONS

Gettin' Down; Gettin' the Blues Blueberries

Beautiful blueberries ripened in time for our annual rain or shine Fourth of July get-together for friends and family in the back yard summerhouse.

Blueberries with Vanilla Almond Yogurt Sauce

The Fruit:

Blueberries, rinsed and patted dry
Bananas, sliced

The Sauce:

¾ cup low-fat plain yogurt
2 tablespoons light brown sugar
½ teaspoon almond extract
1 teaspoon vanilla extract

Combine ingredients and spoon over fruit. This is great on almost any fruit, not just berries and bananas.

Old-Fashioned Summer Pudding
– 4 servings

If, after savoring all those raw blueberries, you'd like to cook some, here's a quick recipe that won't cut into your beach time. We loved making it on Saturday night and having it for Sunday dinner.

2 cups clean, dry blueberries
¼ cup or less to taste granulated sugar
⅓ cup water
4 slices white bread, cut in half and sprinkled
  with cinnamon
Whipped cream
4 individual loaf pans

Toss berries gently with sugar. Bring berries and water to a boil over medium-high heat. Turn heat down to medium and cook, stirring occasionally, 10 minutes. Layer berries and bread in loaf pans, starting with bread and ending with berries. Cover, refrigerate four hours or overnight.

We lavished on the whipped cream and ate right

out of the pan. However, if you want a pretty presentation, put the pudding on a glass plate and add the whipped cream. For a special treat, nestle a scoop of peach ice cream next to the pudding.

Peas
Peas with a Dab of Sweet Butter

This recipe for Art's favorite vegetable, buttered peas, is really no recipe at all. Find somebody who likes to shell peas as much as he did.

Place the shelled peas in a small amount of boiling water and simmer until just tender. Remember overdone peas lose both their color and flavor. Drain peas and serve with a dab of butter and a dash of kosher salt.

Grilled Shrimp on Pasta Salad
with Peas – *4 servings*

The Pasta Salad:

2 cups dry elbow macaroni or pasta of your
   choice
2 tablespoons olive oil
2 tablespoons vinegar
¼ cup sweet onion, finely chopped

½ teaspoon kosher salt
¼ teaspoon black pepper
⅓ cup light mayonnaise
1 cup celery, diced
1½ cups peas, blanched
Parsley for garnish

Cook pasta al dente according to package directions. Rinse under cold water until pasta no longer feels warm. Drain. Drizzle with oil and vinegar. Toss. Add remaining ingredients and toss again gently. Refrigerate until ready to use. Taste and adjust seasonings and mayonnaise if necessary. Garnish with parsley before serving.

The Shrimp:

1 pound large shrimp, peeled, deveined, and cleaned
¼ cup of your favorite vinaigrette dressing
Lemon wedges for garnish

Toss shrimp with the dressing in a small glass bowl. Cover and marinate in the fridge for 45 minutes. Remove shrimp and thread them on skewers. Grill over medium-high heat on a fine wire mesh rack for two minutes on each side just until the shrimp are pink. Remove the shrimp from the skewers and lay them atop the pasta salad, which you have divided among four platters. Garnish with more parsley and the lemon wedges.

Improvise: If you have some peas left, add them to:

Tossed green salad
Fried rice

Buttered carrots
Beef stew
Veggie soup
Noodle soup
Or anything else that sounds good to you

Gettin' a Little Corny

Corn – Keep the ears in a plastic bag in the refrigerator unshucked, until you're ready to cook them. We never had a problem with that. We cooked ours the day Art picked them. After you pull off the green husks, you can either pull the silks off by hand or scrub them off with a stiff wet vegetable brush.

You can freeze corn for up to 6 months. Simply remove it from the cob with a sharp non-carbon knife and pack it in an airtight container or plastic freezer bag.

Boiled Corn

Fresh corn on the cob can be dropped in a pot of water, which is then brought to a boil and boiled for about 3 minutes until just tender. Corn becomes tougher, not softer, when overcooked. If cooking more ears than can be submerged in water, cover the pot so steam can cook the ears on top.

Grilled Corn with Flavored Butter

If you like more of a steamed flavor, grill your corn wrapped in foil or in the husks, but if you go for the flavor of the grill and more sweetness, husk it and follow this recipe. Brush your husked corn generously with flavored butter. Grill over a medium flame about two minutes per side, brushing with more butter as needed. Turn four times so you expose all surfaces to the grill. Serve with additional butter, salt, and pepper.

COOK'S NOTES
IMPROVISATIONS
& VARIATIONS

Flavored Butter

Use your imagination and taste buds to come up with combinations. Here are some to get you started.

Fresh herb butter *– With a wooden spoon, beat a tablespoon of chopped fresh tarragon, thyme, marjoram, chives, cilantro, or parsley into a stick of softened butter.*

Garlic butter *– Substitute 1 or 2 cloves garlic minced for the herbs.*

Scallion butter *– Beat a tablespoon of thinly sliced green scallions into the butter.*

Corn and Black Bean Salad – *4 servings*

2 cups raw corn
1 15 ½ -ounce can black beans, thoroughly
  rinsed and drained
1 cup coarsely chopped fresh tomatoes
½ cup sweet onions, scallions, or a combination
2 tablespoons chopped cilantro
Kosher salt and freshly ground pepper to taste
1 tablespoon fresh lime juice
1 tablespoon white wine vinegar
2 tablespoons extra-virgin olive oil

Combine corn, beans, tomatoes, onions, and cilantro in a bowl. Season to taste with salt and pepper. Mix remaining ingredients in a small bowl or cup and pour over corn mixture. Toss to cover the veggies with the dressing. Allow to sit at room temperature for 30 minutes before serving to bring out the flavors. You can easily turn this into an entrée by topping with grilled shrimp.

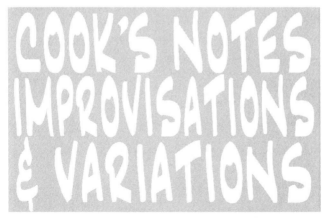

Corn Salad – *4 servings*

4 ears raw corn
1 small red or green bell pepper or a
   combination of both, chopped
2 small to medium ribs celery, thinly sliced
3 scallions, thinly sliced
1 heaping tablespoon chopped cilantro
1 teaspoon white wine vinegar
2 teaspoons fresh lemon juice
3 tablespoons extra-virgin olive oil
¼ heaping teaspoon sugar
½ teaspoon kosher salt
Freshly ground pepper to taste
Juice of ¼ lemon

*Cut the kernels from the cob. Put the corn in a
mixing bowl. Add the bell pepper, celery, scallions,
and cilantro. Toss gently. In a separate small
bowl, whisk together the vinegar, lemon juice, oil,
sugar, salt, and pepper. Pour over the corn mixture
and toss again. Squeeze the juice of ¼ lemon over
all, and toss gently again. Adjust seasonings, if
necessary. Serve at room temperature or chilled.*

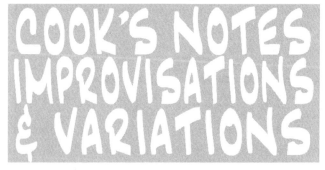

COOK'S NOTES
IMPROVISATIONS
& VARIATIONS

Tomatoes Triumph

Summer Salsa

3 medium tomatoes
Kosher salt to taste
Freshly ground pepper to taste
½ cup sliced scallions
1 ear corn taken off the cob, salted and
  peppered
½ cup chopped green bell pepper
¼ cup chopped cilantro
1 tablespoon chopped green chilies
1 heaping tablespoon finely chopped garlic
Juice of 1 lime
2 tablespoons sugar

Peel and seed the tomatoes. There are various ways to do this. Here's the way I do it. Immerse the tomatoes in boiling water for no more than 30 seconds. Lay them on the counter until they are cool enough to handle. Core them with a paring knife. Peel off the skins by hand. Cut the tomatoes in half and gently squeeze out the seeds.

Chop the tomatoes into a medium bowl. Salt and pepper them. Add remaining ingredients. Mix. Taste for seasonings. Add more salt and pepper, if needed. Cover with plastic wrap and refrigerate two hours. Just before serving, drain and stir gently. If you don't eat it all the first day, you can refrigerate it and serve the rest the next day. Once again, drain before serving.

Fresh Tomato Relish

The Relish

1 large ripe tomato, rinsed and chopped
Garlic powder or minced garlic to taste
Kosher salt to taste
Freshly ground black pepper to taste
½ cup Vidalia onion or scallions, chopped (A
   combination of both is good.)
½ cup green pepper, chopped
2 teaspoons fresh parsley or cilantro, chopped
Put the chopped tomato in a bowl and
   add garlic, salt, pepper. Add remaining
   ingredients.

The Dressing

1 teaspoon cider vinegar (Champagne vinegar
   or white wine vinegar is tasty, too.)
2 ½ teaspoons extra-virgin olive oil

*Mix vinegar and oil and drizzle over the relish.
Toss to coat all the veggies. Serve immediately at
room temperature or refrigerate. If you refrigerate
it, take it out about half an hour before dinner to
enhance the flavors.*

Beets

Spring Mix and Summer Beets – *2 servings*

Spring mix salad greens
4 medium or 8 small cooked beets, sliced,
    salted, and peppered
1 Red Delicious or other sweet eating apple,
    rinsed, thinly sliced, and salted
Blue cheese dressing
Freshly ground pepper to taste
¼ cup coarsely chopped walnuts

*Make a bed of spring mix on each salad plate.
Arrange beets and apples on the bed. Lightly
drizzle with dressing and sprinkle with pepper.
Garnish with walnuts.*

NOTE: Many recipes, especially in older cookbooks,
suggest boiling beets, and that's what I used to do.
This, however, causes the beets to bleed more and
lose nutrients. My favorite cooking method for
beets is microwaving.

*Put on your dollar-store bargain gloves and rinse
the beets gently under running water. Don't use
a vegetable brush; you could break the skins.
Leaving the skins intact helps to prevent loss
of flavor, color and nutrients during cooking.
Place four whole medium or 8 small beets in a
microwave-safe dish. Add a quarter-cup water.
Cover. Cook on high 10 to 20 minutes. Rotate
every five minutes.*

Beets are done when they can be pierced with a

sharp knife. Allow them to stand 3 to 5 minutes before removing them from the water. When they are cool enough to handle with gloved hands, cut the ends off and either remove the skins with a paring knife or by hand. If you are not going to eat them right away, refrigerate peeled beets in a plastic bag until you are ready for them.

COOK'S NOTES IMPROVISATIONS & VARIATIONS

Greens

Greens go great with everything, especially fish and pork. We ate them year 'round.

Sautéed Collard Greens

2 pounds collard greens
2 tablespoons bacon drippings
1 medium Vidalia onion, coarsely chopped
Kosher salt and freshly ground pepper to taste

Hot sauce, cider vinegar, and butter should be available at the table for dinner guests who wish to add them.

Break off and discard the collard stems. Wash the greens thoroughly at least twice to get rid of the grit. The easiest way to do this is to slosh them around in a pan of cool water. The grit will go to the bottom of the pan.

Slice the clean leaves into bite-size pieces, transfer to a pot, cover them with boiling water, and simmer over low heat, just until crisp tender. This can take up to 30 minutes depending on the greens, but check them often. Drain well. Meanwhile, cook the onion in bacon drippings about 3 minutes over medium-high heat. Add the greens, stir, and continue cooking and stirring until the greens are tender to taste. This may take 5 to 10 minutes, according to your preference. Add salt and pepper to taste.

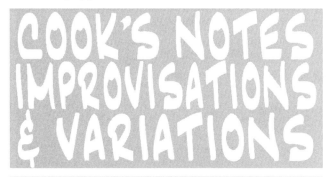

Peaches

Handle ripe peaches with care. They bruise easily so store them side-by-side stem end down in a cool spot. Don't torture them with refrigeration. It diminishes their flavor and juiciness. Wash them gently just before you use them. If you need to cut your peaches a while before serving, squeeze some fresh lemon juice over them to keep them from browning.

Peachy Johnny Cake – *4 servings*

1 pan (8 x 8) of cornbread made from a mix
6 peaches, rinsed, sliced, and sugared to taste
Whipped cream
Fresh blueberries for garnish
Kiwi slices for garnish
Mint sprigs for garnish

*Place a slice of warm cornbread on each of 4
dessert plates. Cover with a layer of whipped
cream. Spoon on a generous serving of juicy
peaches and top the whole thing with more
whipped cream. Blueberries, mint, and kiwi make
a terrific tasty garnish.*

COOK'S NOTES
IMPROVISATIONS
& VARIATIONS

Creamy Peach Pie

¾ cup sugar
¼ cup all purpose flour
¼ teaspoon salt
¼ teaspoon nutmeg
4 cups rinsed, peeled, and sliced peaches
1 cup heavy cream
1 unbaked 9-inch pie shell

Preheat oven to 400 degrees.

Combine sugar, flour, salt and nutmeg. Add to

peaches in a bowl and toss lightly. Arrange in pie shell. Pour heavy cream over peaches. Sprinkle with additional nutmeg if you wish. Bake 45 minutes or until set. Cool before serving.

Note: Pie may be placed on aluminum foil-lined baking sheet. Depending on how juicy the peaches are, they may run over. The baking sheet will protect the oven.

COOK'S NOTES IMPROVISATIONS & VARIATIONS

Peaches Foster – *4 servings*

3 tablespoons butter
1/3 cup brown sugar
1 teaspoon cornstarch
4 rinsed, sliced peaches
2 tablespoons rum or 1 teaspoon rum extract
1 quart vanilla ice cream or yogurt

Melt butter in a glass dish in the microwave. Stir in brown sugar and cornstarch. Add peaches and stir. Microwave uncovered on high 4 minutes, stirring halfway through cooking time. Remove peaches from microwave oven and add rum. Stir. Serve over ice cream.

Improvise: Here are more no-fuss ways to enjoy peaches:

Grill peach halves sprinkled with cinnamon and brown sugar to serve alongside ham, ribs, or chicken.

Fill peach halves with sour cream to which you've added just a dash of almond or vanilla extract. Top with slivered almonds.

Alternate layers of sliced peaches, sugared if necessary, and yogurt or ice cream in champagne glasses.

COOK'S NOTES IMPROVISATIONS & VARIATIONS

Watermelon

I don't think there was a day during watermelon season that we didn't have a big melon in the bottom of the fridge. Art seemed to have a secret knack for picking out the best ones.

Watermelon Salsa – *4 servings*

1 cup cold seedless watermelon balls
1 avocado, diced
¼ cup red or Vidalia onions or scallions, chopped
   (I like to combine onions and scallions.)
4 tablespoons, more or less to taste, cilantro , chopped
2 tablespoons or more to taste fresh lime juice

Kosher salt to taste

Combine ingredients and serve immediately or refrigerate until ready to use.

This partners well with any seafood or chicken entrée.

Watermelon Tomato Salad – *4 servings*

4 tomatoes, rinsed and sliced
2 cups seedless small watermelon balls
¼ cup red or Vidalia onions or scallions,
  chopped (A mixture is really delightful.)
1 tablespoon fresh mint, chopped
1 tablespoon or more to taste fresh lemon juice
1 teaspoon sugar
3 tablespoons extra-virgin olive oil
Kosher salt to taste
Freshly ground black pepper to taste
Fresh mint sprigs for garnish

Line a platter with tomato slices. Layer melon over tomatoes and top with onions and/or scallions. Combine mint, lemon juice, sugar, and oil and drizzle over salad. Salt and pepper to taste. Garnish with mint.

Improvise: If after devouring slices, salads, and salsas, you've still got watermelon left:

Make ice cubes by processing seedless melon in a blender until smooth. Pour into ice cube tray and freeze.

Blend some seedless melon into a fruit smoothie.

Top lemon sorbet with melon balls and garnish with a mint sprig.

Garnish your breakfast, lunch, and dinner plates with wedges of this beautiful, tasty fruit.

COOK'S NOTES IMPROVISATIONS & VARIATIONS

Apples

Chunky Cinnamon Applesauce

Art's favorite fruit side dish was applesauce. He never tasted fresh applesauce until I made it for him. It quickly became a staple in our house.

6 large Granny Smith apples, peeled, cored, and cut into chunks
Kosher salt to taste
Squeeze of fresh lemon juice
3 tablespoons apple juice
1 teaspoon cinnamon
¼ teaspoon ground cloves

¼ teaspoon ground allspice
1 cup sugar or less, if you like a tart taste
Nutmeg to taste

Salt apples and give them a squeeze of lemon juice. Place apples in crockery pot with remaining ingredients, except nutmeg, and mix well. Cover and cook on low 4 hours. Stir. Adjust seasonings, if needed. Sprinkle with nutmeg. Serve warm, room temperature, or cold. It's really good warm as a topping for vanilla ice cream, too.

COOK'S NOTES
IMPROVISATIONS
& VARIATIONS

Cinnamon Apple Loaf

½ cup butter, softened
¾ cup sugar
1 large egg
1¼ cups chunky cinnamon applesauce
1½ cups all-purpose flour
1½ teaspoons baking soda
½ teaspoon ground cinnamon
¾ teaspoon ground nutmeg
¼ teaspoon ground cloves
½ teaspoon salt
½ cup chopped walnuts

Preheat oven to 350 degrees.

In mixing bowl cream butter and sugar. Add egg and applesauce. Mix well. In a separate bowl, combine flour, baking soda, cinnamon, nutmeg, and cloves. Add salt. Gradually add this mixture to the applesauce mixture, stirring just until combined. Fold in nuts. Pour into greased 8-inch by 4-inch loaf pan. Bake for 50 minutes or until toothpick inserted near center comes out clean. Cool for 10 minutes before removing from pan to wire rack to cool more. This is good served alone, with soft cream cheese, or accompanied by a dab of whipped cream.

COOK'S NOTES IMPROVISATIONS & VARIATIONS

Autumn Apple Pudding – *6 servings*

½ cup flour
1 cup brown sugar
1 teaspoon cinnamon
5 large Granny Smith apples, peeled, and thinly sliced
¼ cup butter, sliced into pats
1 cup sour cream
1 cup graham cracker crumbs

Preheat oven to 375 degrees.

Mix flour, sugar, and cinnamon. Combine the mixture thoroughly with the apples. Transfer ingredients to a lightly buttered casserole dish. Lay butter pats on top of mixture. Spread sour cream over mixture. Sprinkle graham cracker crumbs on top. Bake 30 minutes or until apples are just crisp tender.

COOK'S NOTES IMPROVISATIONS & VARIATIONS

Cranberries

Cranberry Orange Sauce – *6 servings*

2¼ cups fresh cranberries, rinsed and drained
1 cup sugar
¾ cup orange marmalade
1 tablespoon fresh lemon juice
1 tablespoon brandy, optional but highly
  recommended

Preheat oven to 350 degrees.

Toss cranberries and sugar. Add marmalade and lemon juice. Place in buttered 1-quart baking dish. Cover. Bake 1 hour. (If adding brandy, do so after 40 minutes.) Remove from oven and uncover dish. Allow to sit on the counter to thicken 45 minutes if serving as a side dish.

Note: If you love ice cream sundaes, waste no time in topping vanilla ice cream with the cranberry concoction. You can do this as quickly as 15 minutes after it comes out of the oven. The taste is absolutely glorious.

Crockery Cranberry Sauce – *About 3 cups*

Art had tasted cranberry sauce only from the can until we started making our own. After that, he never bought another jar of the jellied stuff again.

1 12-ounce package fresh cranberries
2 cups sugar
¼ cup water

Pick over the cranberries, rinse them, and drain. Combine cranberries with sugar and water in crockery pot. Cover and cook on high 3½ hours. Serve hot or cold.

Note: The cranberries will keep in a covered container for up to 3 weeks in the refrigerator and up to 2 months in the freezer.

Goin' Nutty: Gettin' Crabby and Shy

Art's Nutty Shrimp – *4 servings*

This is a takeoff on a shrimp casserole Art was fed at a fan's house in New Orleans.

4 -ounces elbow macaroni
¼ cup butter
½ cup, more or less, blanched almonds, slivered
¼ cup green pepper, chopped (If you have a
  red pepper in the fridge, use a combination of
  green and red.)
¼ cup flour
2 cups milk
1 to 1½ cups medium shrimp, cooked and cleaned
Buttered bread crumbs

Preheat oven to 350 degrees.

Cook macaroni according to package directions until tender but firm.

Melt butter in sauce pan over low heat. Add almonds and green pepper and cook over medium heat for a minute.

Stir in the flour. Then gently add the milk and continue cooking until thick. Stay with it and stir it often as it thickens.

Put the elbows and shrimp in a 1 ½ quart baking dish. Pour the sauce over and mix. Top with buttered bread crumbs.

Bake about 25 minutes until top is nicely browned. Don't bake it too long; the shrimp will get tough.

Our Crabby Creole Casserole – *4 servings*

One night when we really wanted to go over to the Captain's Galley for some saucy sole, a nor'easter kept us housebound. So we made a crab casserole from what was on hand. After a couple glasses of wine, we mellowed out and enjoyed the crab.

2 tablespoons butter
¼ cup onion, chopped
1 clove garlic, minced
½ medium green pepper, chopped
1 tablespoon flour
1 14½ -ounce can stewed or diced tomatoes
1 teaspoon sugar
1 pound cooked crab meat
Buttered bread crumbs

Preheat oven to 350 degrees.

Melt butter in skillet over low heat. Turn heat up to medium and saute' onion, garlic, and green pepper for three minutes. Remove from heat and add flour. Return to heat. Sugar the tomatoes and add them to the pan. Simmer about 20 minutes. Add crab meat and put in baking dish. Top with buttered bread crumbs.

Bake for 15 minutes or so until crab is heated through. Serve with a bottle of Louisiana hot sauce.

COOK'S NOTES IMPROVISATIONS & VARIATIONS

Art's Nutty Chicken – *4 servings*

2 cups, more or less, leftover roast chicken, cubed
2 stalks celery, chopped
½ cup, more or less, blanched almonds, slivered
Freshly ground black pepper to taste
1 tablespoon or more onion, chopped
3 tablespoons finely chopped sweet pickles or well drained pickle relish
1 cup, more or less, mayonnaise
Grated cheese of your choice for topping (Art used hot pepper cheese when he had it.)
Crushed potato chips or corn flakes for topping

Preheat oven to 350 degrees.

Put everything except cheese and chips in bowl and mix. Pour into 1½ quart casserole. Top with cheese and chips. Bake until heated through and browned a little. This will probably take about 30 minutes.

Art's Amateur Shrimp Etouffee – *4 servings*

Art, always outgoing, really was shy about making this because we'd eaten so much etouffee in New Orleans where it had been perfected. Actually, his wouldn't deserve a drum roll, but it was O.K. and sooo easy to make.

2 tablespoons butter plus more as needed
2 medium green peppers, chopped
1 large sweet onion, chopped
1 stalk celery, chopped
1 clove garlic
2 pounds shrimp, peeled and cleaned
2 tablespoons tomato paste, catsup, or chili
  sauce
Wine, chicken broth, or water as needed
Green onion tops, sliced for garnish

Melt butter in skillet over low heat. Add peppers, onion, celery, and garlic and cook over medium heat a few minutes until tender. Add more butter if needed. Add shrimp and tomato paste. Turn heat to low, cover pan, and cook just until shrimp are heated through. Don't let them overcook and get tough. If you need a little more liquid along the way, add some wine, chicken broth, or water.

Serve garnished with green onion tops (scallions) accompanied by rice and a bottle of Louisiana Hot Sauce.

COOK'S NOTES IMPROVISATIONS & VARIATIONS

Hurricanes

Music permeated every room of our house. We had a great sound system in the den, and when we cranked up the volume and opened the French doors that led to the living room, you could hear it all over the downstairs. I also had a little record player in a beige suitcase I took from room to room. Takashi mixed, Art chopped, and I simmered to jazz, funk, R&B, gospel, blues, traditional....

I'd be lifting the lid on the creole pork chops with the Preservation Hall Jazz Band playing "The Bucket's Got a Hole in It," and Art would come gliding down the staircase singing along with Takashi's little red umbrella in one hand and a white hanky twirling in the other. He'd throw some beads my way. We'd both have a big grin on our face and go dancin' around the dining room table. We'd end up back in the kitchen and Art would make us a Pat O'Brien's Hurricane. A few days later, we'd do it all again to the sounds of the Olympic Brass Band's "Didn't He Ramble." Some things really are worth repeating.

Hurricanes, by the way, were created by trial and error at Pat O'Brien's place in New Orleans during World War II when liquor, especially bourbon and scotch, was in short supply. The good news was that rum came up the river in great supply. The downside was that bar owners were forced to buy about 50 cases at a time.

As they say, necessity is the mother of invention. So with the help of an eager salesman, the staff at Pat O'Brien's came up with a new drink to use up some of that rum. Legend is they served the fruity concoction in a hurricane lamp shaped glass, and somebody said, "That's it; let's call it a Hurricane." Voila!

I don't drink anymore, but I still go to Pat O'Brien's for the fried catfish and crawfish etouffee. Usually, I'm the only person in the courtyard not downing a Hurricane. But I'm having as much fun as anybody, toe tapping to the music and remembering.

In a 26-ounce Hurricane glass mix 4 -ounces Pat O'Brien's Hurricane Rum or any good dark rum and 4 -ounces Pat O'Brien's Hurricane Mix available by mail at 1-800-597-4823. Fill the glass with crushed ice and garnish with orange slices and a cherry.

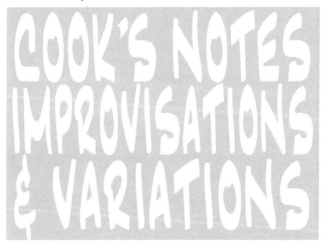

COOK'S NOTES IMPROVISATIONS & VARIATIONS

The Soup Pot
aka The Crock Pot

Soup is reliable, and in that alone we find a certain amount of comfort.

Deborah Madison, Cookbook Writer

Art saw soup as one of life's comfortable constants, nourishment for both body and soul. He never forgot that Sara Perran always had a soup pot on the stove when he was growing up. Usually it was vegetable soup made of whatever her employer had thrown out that day. She would forage through the garbage, salvage what she could, and take it home, where she miraculously turned it into a palatable supper for her children.

Every week we accumulated vegetables, bones, and meat and simmered them into soup. Art would get into a rhythm slicing and chopping, and I'd put it all together with some seasonings in the crockery pot. The house would be filled with the most enticing aroma all day long.

Every time I read Billy Collins' poem *I Chop Some Parsley While Listening to Art Blakey's Version of "Three Blind Mice,"* I smile and for a wonderful moment am transported back to the yellow kitchen on Mill Road. Art is at the counter chopping sweet Vidalia onions, and the sun is pouring in the big window over the sink.

Being a lover of everything Italian, Art introduced me

to the "lentil soup on New Year's Day" tradition. Some time near the end of the old year, he'd go out and buy a beautiful ham for baking. He'd score it and I'd top it with cloves and a brown sugar mixture. The most wonderful scent would come from the oven. Then after dinner, he'd tuck the leftover ham and the bone away for New Year's Day soup.

On Easter we'd have ham too, and after the leftover meat and bone were resting in the fridge, our thoughts would turn to the rich barley soup we'd make the next day. Even when Easter comes late in the spring, nights are cool and it's still soup weather in New Jersey.

Sometimes we'd take the leftover ham and instead of adding barley, we'd cook it up with lima beans. Our lima bean soup was so thick, it was like a stew. Art liked soup thick, and I understood why. Growing up as poor as he did, what broth there was often had to be thinned so there would be enough to go around. Seconds were unheard of.

Sundays we often had chicken for dinner. Art would cut the leftover chicken off the bones and store it in a plastic bag beside the carcass in the fridge, the start of yet another soup. He was so precise and saved every single bite of meat. Nothing was wasted – a habit, I am sure, learned of necessity early in life. Kitchen work never really seemed like work for him. It was his way of relaxing, and it always made him smile.

Hearty Crockery Pot Lentil Soup
– 4 large servings

1½ cups lentils, rinsed
6 cups water plus 3 cups water
1 8 -ounce can tomato sauce
1 tablespoon sugar
1 small ham bone or pork hock
Kosher salt, pepper, garlic powder
1 medium onion, diced
2 carrots, thinly sliced
2 stalks celery, thinly sliced
Leftover finely diced ham

Precook lentils in 6 cups water in covered crockery pot set on low overnight. The next morning drain the lentils and discard the water. Place the lentils, ham bone or pork hock, tomato sauce, and sugar in the crockery pot. Season to taste with salt, pepper, and garlic powder. Add 3 cups water. Stir.

Saute' carrots, onion, and celery in a little oil over medium heat for 5 minutes. Add to the pot. Stir. Adjust seasonings. Add diced ham. Cook covered on low 6-8 hours. Remove ham bone or pork hock after two hours. Adjust seasonings if necessary before serving.

Note: Serve this with crusty Italian bread and salad. What a great start to the New Year.

Jazzed-Up Lima Bean Soup
– 4 large servings

1 pound dry lima beans
1 large onion, coarsely chopped
1 large green pepper, coarsely chopped
¼ pound ham, cut into small pieces
1 10½ -ounce can tomato soup
1 can water (10½ -ounces)
Kosher salt, pepper, and garlic powder to taste

Soak the beans overnight according to package directions. Combine all ingredients in crockery pot and stir. Cover and cook on low 8 hours or until beans are tender. Adjust seasonings as necessary.

This thick soup tastes even better when served with warm muffins or hearty bread.

COOK'S NOTES
IMPROVISATIONS
& VARIATIONS

Crockery Navy Bean Soup
– 4 generous servings

1 16 -ounce package navy beans
6 cups water
1 14½ -ounce can whole tomatoes, broken up
  by hand
1 heaping tablespoon tightly packed light
  brown sugar
2 tablespoons white vinegar

1 teaspoon kosher salt
½ teaspoon pepper
1 cup diced ham
2 tablespoons chopped onion
2 packets Goya ham flavored seasoning or ham
  bone

The night before, rinse and pick over the beans. Place the beans and water in the crockery pot, and cook covered on low overnight, about 10 hours. In the morning, stir the beans. Combine the tomatoes, sugar, vinegar, salt, and pepper, and add to the beans. Stir. Add the ham, onion, and ham seasoning or ham bone. Stir again. Cook covered on low until beans are tender, about 6 to 8 hours. Check seasonings and add more salt and pepper to taste, if needed.

Crockery Ham and Barley Soup
– 4 large servings

1 ham bone
1½ cups tomato juice
3 cups water
1 14½ -ounce can undrained tomatoes
1 14½ -ounce can drained green beans
2 thinly sliced celery stalks
1 thinly sliced carrot
1 small chopped onion

½ cup barley (Use medium pearl, not quick-
   cooking barley.)
1 1.31 -ounce package McCormick Sloppy Joe
   Seasoning Mix
Kosher salt, pepper, and garlic powder to taste

*Combine all ingredients and cook covered in the
crockery pot on low 6 to 8 hours. Remove the ham
bone after 5 hours, cut off the meat, and put meat
back in the pot.*

Crockery Vegetable Beef Soup
– 4 to 6 extra-large servings

1 28 -ounce can tomatoes, broken up with your
   hands
2 tablespoons sugar
2 carrots, sliced
2 medium potatoes, peeled and diced
1 medium onion, coarsely chopped
1 14½ -ounce can cut green beans, drained
1 15¼ -ounce can corn, drained
2 cups beef broth
½ cup tomato juice
½ pound stewing beef, cut into small bites
Salt, pepper, and garlic powder to taste

*Combine tomatoes and sugar. Put all ingredients
into crockery pot and stir. Cover. Cook on low 7 to*

9 hours. If you're away from the house and need to let it cook longer, don't worry. It'll be just as tasty after 10 hours. Check for seasonings before serving.

Note: This soup is really good with French or Italian bread, but crackers will do just fine. You can jazz it up by replacing one of the white potatoes with a sweet potato. That's what my friend Harriet Feldman used to do. She learned it from her dad, Sidney. Also try adding a turnip or parsnip, and if you've got a head of cabbage, chop some and throw it in too, an hour before the soup is done.

Variations: If you've got some leftover baked ham, roast beef, or corned beef in the fridge, add it the last hour and omit the stewing beef.

To make Vegetable Beef Barley Soup, add 1/3 cup medium pearl barley to the original ingredients. Don't use quick-cooking barley.

For Vegetable Beef Macaroni Soup, add a cup of cooked al dente elbow or other macaroni to the pot just before serving. Add cooked noodles before serving, and voila! You've got Vegetable Beef Noodle soup.

For Chicken Vegetable Soup, substitute chicken broth and chicken pieces for the beef broth and the stewing beef.

Beefy Cabbage Soup
– 4 to 6 extra large servings

1 28 -ounce can tomatoes in tomato juice, broken up by hand
4 tablespoons brown or white sugar
½ pound beef stew cubes, cut into bite-size pieces
2 carrots, sliced
2 medium potatoes, peeled and diced
1 medium onion, coarsely chopped
1 14½ -ounce can green beans, drained
2 to 3 cups beef broth
Kosher salt, pepper, and garlic powder to taste
2 cups green cabbage, coarsely chopped

Combine tomatoes with sugar. Pour into crockery pot. Add remaining ingredients except cabbage. Stir. Cover. Cook on low 6 to 8 hours. As with most vegetable soups, it will be just fine if you're away and need to let it cook 10 hours. However long you cook it, don't add the cabbage until the last hour. Check for seasonings before serving.

Leave the crackers on the shelf and serve this with Italian bread.

COOK'S NOTES IMPROVISATIONS & VARIATIONS

Day After Thanksgiving
Turkey Noodle Soup

Turkey carcass
2 celery stalks, sliced
1 large onion, coarsely chopped
4 carrots, sliced
1 turnip, chopped
2 potatoes, peeled and chopped
Kosher salt, pepper, and garlic powder to taste
1 cup cooked noodles

Place carcass in crockery pot and cover with water. Add celery stalks and onion. Cook on low 8 to 10 hours. Remove the carcass and put the meat from the carcass back into the pot. Add carrots, turnip, and potatoes. Cook covered on low 6 hours. Add salt, pepper, and garlic powder to taste. Add cooked noodles just before serving.

Variation: Use chicken in place of turkey. Now you've got everybody's favorite chicken noodle soup.

Crockery Chicken Pasta Soup – *4 servings*

8 baby carrots, thinly sliced
2 stalks celery, thinly sliced
1 small onion, chopped
1 15¼ -ounce can white corn, drained
4 cups chicken stock
Kosher salt, pepper, and garlic powder
1 cup cubed cooked chicken
8 -ounces dry small pasta shells, cooked and
   drained
4 scallions, sliced

Put carrots, celery, onion, and corn in crockery pot.
Add chicken stock. Add kosher salt, pepper and
garlic powder to taste. Cover. Cook on low 6 to 8
hours. Add chicken and shells. Adjust seasonings.
Serve garnished with sliced scallions.

COOK'S NOTES
IMPROVISATIONS
& VARIATIONS

Pasta e Fagioli – *4 extra-large servings*

Olive oil
½ pound hot or mild Italian sausage
1 28 -ounce can crushed tomatoes in puree,
   peppered, salted, and garlic powdered
1 cup tomato juice
4 tablespoons sugar

1 medium onion, coarsely chopped
1 cup celery, chopped
1 carrot, thinly sliced and salted
1 15½ -ounce can cannellini beans(white kidney
  beans), rinsed, drained,
  salted, peppered, and garlic powered
1 7 -ounce package elbow macaroni, cooked al
  dente

*Heat a sauté pan over a medium- high burner.
Pour in a small amount of oil. Add sausage,
breaking it up as you brown it.*

*Meanwhile, combine seasoned tomatoes, tomato
juice, and sugar in crockery pot.*

*Drain the sausage on a paper towel and add it to
the pot.*

*Add remaining ingredients except pasta. Cover.
Cook on low 5 to 8 hours, depending on how
crunchy you like your veggies.*

*Just before serving, cook the pasta, drain it, and
spoon it into large soup bowls. Pour the soup over it.*

Serve with a big basket of Italian bread.

Somebody said there are as many recipes for pasta
e fagioli as there are cooks. I think, as with most soups,
cooks use what's on hand.

My friend Nick Regine, who's been eating pasta e fagioli
all his life, adds a splash of white wine to his soup and
serves it over bow tie pasta. Think I'll try that next time.

COOK'S NOTES
IMPROVISATIONS
& VARIATIONS

Corn Chowder – *4 generous servings*

In Winchester, Indiana, where I was raised, everybody either had a garden or lived next door to somebody who did, and they all planted sweet corn. So why did I have to wait to taste my first bowl of corn chowder when I grew up and ventured down to New Orleans?

I still don't know the answer to that. Indiana cooks, if you're reading this, I'm begging you to add this delightful easy to make corn soup to your repertoire and pass on the recipe to all your foodie friends. Anne Riddle, how about giving out corn chowder recipes at the Winchester farmers market? Hoosiers, it's not too late to make up for this oversight of past generations.

I don't remember the name of the tiny mom and pop restaurant where I first ate this gift from the gods, and I didn't even ask for the recipe. But that's all right because I don't think there ever was a written recipe. They cooked strictly from the heart and soul.

Anyway, here's my crockery pot version which I made year-round. In the summer, I used fresh corn Art had picked that morning on a nearby farm, and in the winter, I switched to frozen corn.

1 cup onions, finely chopped
1 cup carrots, thinly sliced
1 cup celery, finely chopped
½ cup green or red peppers or a combination
2 cups potatoes, peeled, finely chopped, and

peppered

2½ to 3 cups fresh or frozen corn, peppered

1 14.75 -ounce can cream style corn, peppered

1 to 1½ cups chicken broth

1½ cups heavy cream

Freshly ground pepper to taste

Louisiana hot sauce to taste

Green onions (scallions), finely chopped for
  garnish

*Put everything except the cream, hot sauce, and
green onions in the crockery pot. Stir. Cover. Cook
on low 5 to 7 hours.*

*Add the cream. Stir again and put the lid back on.
You can serve it as soon as it is heated through or
keep it covered on low setting if you're not quite
ready to eat yet. Before serving, taste it and check
the seasoning. Add more pepper if needed. Add
hot sauce to your liking. We liked a lot. Top each
bowl with chopped green onions.*

*Don't even think about serving this with crackers.
It deserves the best French or Italian bread you can
find.*

Note: Work some magic. Turn this into corn bacon
chowder by adding six slices of cooked, diced
bacon before serving or change it into corn shrimp
chowder by adding cooked, peeled, chopped
shrimp the last few minutes of cooking time.

Take it up another notch by adding both shrimp
and crab meat. Now you've got seafood corn
chowder. And don't forget you've probably got

some leftover roast chicken in the fridge or freezer if you want to morph it into chicken corn chowder. Just shred or chop some white meat and add it the last few minutes of cooking time.

Whichever way you dance this dance, have fun and savor the flavor with people you love.

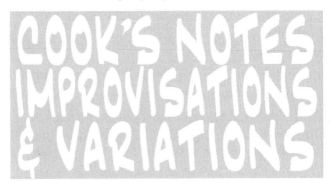

COOK'S NOTES
IMPROVISATIONS
& VARIATIONS

Cooking by Light Bulb and Other Gastronomical Fetes

Love is feeding everybody.

John Denver, Singer, Songwriter

Our love of food and cooking was not lost on Takashi. His foray into the kitchen began at age 7 when I bought him a slightly used yellow Easy-Bake oven for Christmas.

I got it from Doc Brown, the neighborhood chiropractor, who was grateful to unload the little appliance. It had, after all, been sitting in the middle of his home office with a sale sign on it since Labor Day. Over the summer it had become evident neither of his children had even the slightest interest in becoming a home chef. When we closed the cash deal on the Easy-Bake, he even threw in a dozen minuscule boxes of mixes.

On Christmas morning Takashi immediately took to the light-bulb-powered appliance and concocted a yellow cake slathered with chocolate frosting. This was followed by an impromptu but formal afternoon tea for his Aunt Jane, Aunt Devi, and me, featuring miniature chocolate chip cookies and brownies served on the elegant mahogany dining room table. We all put on our best manners and smiled gratefully, in the hope this pampering would never end.

Indeed, over the next few months, our little chef continued to turn out tasty selections of frosted chocolate, white, and yellow cakes; chocolate chip cookies embellished with M&Ms; and a deluxe version of nut brownies. Then something happened we hadn't bargained for. He tired of shelling out 88 cents for the teeny mixes. After he couldn't talk the company into giving him a bulk discount, he did what any smart businessperson would do. He retired the "little oven that could" to his upstairs bedroom and graduated to the full-size Kenmore gas kitchen range, where he no longer had to pay for his ingredients. Everything he needed was in the cupboard right next to the oven.

He was a natural in the kitchen. He made up recipes for strawberry salad and other delights before he could spell the words. On October 11, he prepared tacos and cake for Art's birthday. Art proclaimed that without a doubt, it was the sweetest birthday he'd ever celebrated in all his 58 years.

Come November, our little chef, at age 8, cooked the entire barbequed ribs Thanksgiving dinner for ten of us. I still wish Art could have been there for that. But the reality of living with a jazz musician is that jazz clubs rarely if ever close for this or any other holiday. The only assistance Takashi required with the meal was a little help sounding out some of the words in the recipes.

Strawberry Spinach Salad – *4 servings*

The salad

4 cups fresh torn spinach, rinsed and patted dry
1 cup fresh strawberries, rinsed, patted dry and
halved with tops removed (Reserve 4 whole
berries with tops on for garnish.)
½ cup thinly sliced red onions, separated into
rings
¼ cup pitted black olives
Freshly ground black pepper to taste

Toss salad. Top with pepper to taste.

The dressing:

*This is a basic vinaigrette dressing we used for
most salads. It's simple. Combine 3 parts extra-
virgin olive oil with 1 part vinegar. Add salt and
pepper to taste.*

The presentation: Place the salad on 4 plates. Put a
whole strawberry in the center of each serving.

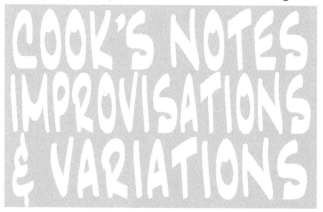

COOK'S NOTES
IMPROVISATIONS
& VARIATIONS

Takashi's Tacos – *4 servings*

The Filling:

1 pound lean ground beef (chuck, round, or sirloin)
1 teaspoon oregano
1 teaspoon ground cumin
1 teaspoon salt
1 teaspoon chili powder
½ teaspoon pepper
8 -ounces taco sauce
8 taco shells

The Toppings:

Shredded extra- sharp cheddar, Monterey Jack, or other cheese of your choice
Shredded cabbage
Chopped cilantro
Sliced green onions
Diced fresh tomatoes
Sour cream

Brown beef over medium to medium-high heat. Add seasonings. Turn heat to low. Add taco sauce. Cover and simmer 15 minutes. Fill shells with meat mixture. Top to taste.

COOK'S NOTES IMPROVISATIONS & VARIATIONS

Apples on the Bottom Cake

This is the moist, gooey delight Takashi baked for Art's 58th birthday.

Topping on the Bottom:

2 Granny Smith apples, rinsed, peeled and sliced
3 tablespoons melted butter
²/₃ cup brown sugar

Sauté apples in butter and brown sugar over medium heat. Transfer to a greased 13" x 9" cake pan.

Cake:

1 box 18.25 -ounce yellow cake mix(I prefer
  Betty Crocker Super Moist.)

Preheat oven to 350 degrees.

Mix the batter according to box directions and spread the batter over the apples. Bake according to box directions. Let it stand 10 minutes after removing it from the oven. Serve it warm while you sing a rousing verse of "Happy Birthday."

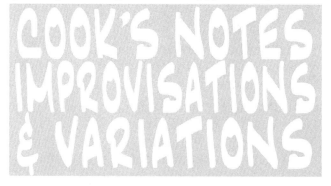

COOK'S NOTES IMPROVISATIONS & VARIATIONS

Barbeque Sauce – *Makes about 2½ cups*

4 tablespoons melted butter
2 medium onions, chopped
Garlic powder to taste
1 cup catsup
4 teaspoons vinegar
1 teaspoon Tabasco sauce
3 tablespoons brown sugar
2 teaspoons salt
2 teaspoons dry mustard
3 tablespoons Worcestershire sauce

Sauté onions in butter over medium heat until just soft, not brown. Transfer to saucepan, add remaining ingredients and bring to a boil.

Barbequed Country Ribs – *4-6 servings*

3½ pounds bone-in country pork ribs
Salt, pepper, garlic powder to taste
Barbeque sauce
Preheat oven to 425 degrees.

Place seasoned ribs in roasting pan and bake 10 minutes on each side. Transfer ribs to crockery pot, pour sauce over them and cook covered on low

6 to 8 hours until tender. Serve with some warm sauce on the side or drizzled lightly over the ribs just before serving.

Note: Takashi made these ribs year 'round, not just at Thanksgiving. They're good over yellow rice.

Cole Slaw for Aunt Jane – *6 servings*

1 cup Hellman's mayonnaise
3 tablespoons fresh lemon juice
2 tablespoons sugar
1 teaspoon kosher salt
6 cups shredded green and red cabbage
1 cup carrots, peeled and shredded
¼ cup scallions, thinly sliced

In a larger bowl, combine first 4 ingredients. Add remaining ingredients and mix well. Refrigerate until ready to serve. Stir before serving.

Cole Slaw for Aunt Devi – *6 servings*

The Dressing:

1½ cups extra- virgin olive oil
½ cup vinegar
Salt, pepper to taste

Mix ingredients.

The Slaw:

6 cups shredded red and green cabbage
½ cup chopped parsley
½ cup chopped green and red peppers

*Pour as much dressing over slaw as needed. Stir.
Refrigerate until ready to serve. Use the leftover
dressing for tomorrow's tossed salad.*

Veggies and Dip Platter

When Takashi cooked, this is the platter that always
served as the centerpiece on the dining room table.

The Veggies:

Broccoli florets
Cauliflower florets
Carrots sticks
Others of your choice

The Dip:

Simply add curry powder to taste to mayonnaise. Put it in a pretty little glass bowl and surround it with the vegetables.

Apples 'n' Sweets – *6 servings*

2 Granny Smith apples, rinsed and sliced
½ cup brown sugar
½ teaspoon cinnamon
Dash of nutmeg
2 16 -ounce cans sweet potatoes, drained
¼ cup butter
2 cups, or less to taste, miniature marshmallows
  (optional)

Preheat oven to 350 degrees.

Toss apples with brown sugar, cinnamon, and nutmeg. Alternate layers of apple mixture and sweet potatoes in 1½-quart casserole. Dot with butter. Cover. Bake 35 minutes. If you wish, top with marshmallows and broil until lightly browned.

Frozen Cranberry Pineapple Salad
– 6 servings

1 16 -ounce can whole berry cranberry sauce
1 20½ -ounce can crushed pineapple, well
  drained
1 cup light sour cream

*Mix ingredients thoroughly. Pour into a mold or
other container. Freeze at least 3 hours until firm.
Thirty minutes before serving, transfer the salad to
the refrigerator.*

Maple Squash Pie – *6 servings*

3 eggs, slightly beaten
½ cup sugar
½ cup maple syrup
½ teaspoon cinnamon
½ teaspoon ginger
½ teaspoon salt
2 12 -ounce packages frozen squash, thawed
1 cup light cream
9 inch unbaked pie shell
½ cup heavy cream, whipped
½ cup maple syrup for drizzling

Heat oven to 400 degrees.

Make filling: In large bowl, combine eggs, sugar, maple syrup, spices, salt, squash, and light cream. Beat with rotary beater until smooth. Turn most of filling into unbaked pie shell. Place on lowest shelf of oven; pour in rest of filling. Bake 55 to 60 minutes, or until filling is set in center when pie is gently shaken. Let cool on wire rack. Serve pie slightly warm or cold. Garnish with whipped cream rosettes, drizzled with maple syrup.

Aunt Jane Stuff

No chapter on Takashi's culinary adventures would be complete without homage to his Aunt Jane, a born cook. He learned the true meaning of home cooking from her, including how to make the world's best scalloped potatoes. She also taught him how to get the chef at McGee's Restaurant in Atlantic City to reveal his secret cheesecake recipe. To this day, the cheesy potatoes and creamy cheesecake are staples at our family gatherings.

Scalloped Potatoes – *4 servings*

2 pounds potatoes (about 6)
3 tablespoons butter
3 tablespoons flour
Salt/pepper to taste
2½ cups milk
¼ cup finely chopped onion
1 tablespoon butter
16 -ounces shredded extra-sharp cheese

Preheat oven to 350 degrees.

Peel potatoes, cut into thin slices, parboil.

Sauce:

Melt 3 tablespoons butter in saucepan. Blend in flour, seasonings. Cook till smooth and bubbly. Remove from heat. Stir in milk. Heat to boiling, stirring constantly. Boil and stir 1 minute.

Grease 2-quart casserole dish. Arrange potatoes, sauce, cheese, onion in layers (top layer should be cheese). Bake 30 minutes in covered dish. Uncover. Bake 60-70 minutes longer until tender. Let stand 5 to 10 minutes before serving.

COOK'S NOTES
IMPROVISATIONS
& VARIATIONS

McGee's Cheesecake

¾ cup sugar
½ pint whipping cream
16 -ounces cream cheese, softened
1 teaspoon vanilla
1 graham cracker crust

Beat sugar and cream together. Add cream cheese and vanilla. Mix. Pour into crust. Chill at least one hour.

COOK'S NOTES IMPROVISATIONS & VARIATIONS

Jack Whittemore, Art's
booking agent and
earth angel.

Photos courtesy of
Nancy Maccini, Jack
Whittemore's daughter,
who I came to know and
love during the writing
of this book.

Christmas Cookies for a Wise Man

Food – God's love made edible

Brother Thomas, the Nada Hermitage

This chapter is lovingly dedicated posthumously to Jack Whittemore's daughter, Nancy Maccini, who died January 25, 2008 while this book was in progress. I know her beautiful spirit is reading every word.

The major recipient of Takashi's Christmas baking was Jack Whittemore. To simply say that Jack was Art's booking agent would be way more than an understatement. Jack, the calmest, gentlest soul I'd ever known since my Grandma Warren, was Art's father confessor, mediator, personal banker, best friend, and fan. He was part of our extended family, our wise man, our sage, and Takashi and I loved him as dearly as Art did. He had, after all, saved my life when he helped me leave Art and go to Atlantic City that painful October day in 1973.

As for Takashi, Jack was the adoring uncle who always made time for him. If Jack had to tend to business on the phone, he'd give Takashi his own pad and pencil to occupy him. Since he was a toddler, Takashi's passion had been drawing. He never traveled anywhere without his drawing pad, a box of Crayolas, and a couple of pencils. But when he was at Jack's, he preferred to use the pencil and paper Jack provided. It was a connection, a ritual between them.

As soon as Jack could break away from business he'd get back to Takashi, and they'd pour over the pictures and laugh and talk together. Jack saved everything in a manila folder.

Takashi still remembers with a chuckle another routine they had. This one centered around Jack's glass-topped table. Between the two layers of glass, Jack would line up Hershey kisses. Then he'd direct Takashi to crawl under the table, rescue and devour them. When the chocolates were all gone, they'd nod and smile knowingly at one another.

Except for his broad shoulders, Jack was a small man of slight build, only five feet six inches. By the time I knew him, his soft, short-cropped hair was gray. Most of his impeccably fitting suits were gray, too. His ties were thin, some striped, others floral.

You never wondered whether Jack was paying attention when you spoke. His intense brown eyes assured you he was listening. He didn't have even an ounce of fat anywhere, which was really amazing because he hadn't exercised since he was an awesome soccer player growing up in Ridgewood, New Jersey. His skin was smooth, his face unwrinkled, and he never looked like he needed a shave.

Besides Art, Jack booked Amad Jamal, Stan Getz and others. Probably if he'd had just Art or Stan and nobody else, it still would have been a full-time job.

In my early years with Art, he had a reputation for not showing up on time for gigs, shorting band members on their pay when he got around to paying them at all, stiffing the second-class hotels that didn't have the forethought to charge him in advance, and borrowing money from both friends and strangers that he never intended to repay. Heroin demanded and took a big chunk of his income.

Sometimes he'd end up unannounced at Jack's at 4 a.m. Without preaching, Jack listened and helped to pick up the pieces and glue them back together. He didn't need to write anything down; he filed things in his head. He'd make a mental note to call Max Gordon at the Vanguard and assure him Art would show up for the second set as well as the opening and closing sets Thursday night. He'd put a twenty-dollar bill in an envelope for Carter Jefferson, the current sax player, to pick up from the doorman later. That would tide him over until Sunday night's payday, which Art promised him he would meet this time.

Art was an equal opportunity employer, especially when he was high on heroin and drunk. He invited pretty women who came to his gigs to travel the country with him and gave wanna-be roadies promises of jobs managing the band. When they took him seriously and showed up with suitcases in hand, he usually had no memory of them. Their images had faded from his head as the night's heroin and vodka wore off. Jack would routinely provide them with carfare back home, wherever that was.

Art was forever in conflict with club owners, promoters, the Internal Revenue Service, and anybody who naively extended him credit. He mismanaged the money his addiction didn't swallow. He didn't pay taxes, and got so many draws during the week that often club owners wouldn't owe him much by closing night. Even after the government seized his apartment building at 415 Central Park West for back taxes in the 1950's, he still made no effort to settle with the IRS.

Since Art was on the road much of the time and, even with the best of intentions, couldn't be trusted to find his way to a post office or Western Union, Jack sent me a monthly check to cover rent and utilities on our Mill Road house. When Art got a lucrative tour in Japan or Europe, Jack would repay himself. He never charged Art a penny of interest and he never missed a month sending me the payment.

Jack worked all his magic from the living-room-turned-office in his small beige-on-beige one-bedroom apartment at 80 Park Avenue. The office was officially open from 10 a.m. to 6 p.m. Monday through Friday, including most holidays. But no musician ever got turned away no matter what time he called or showed up with a sad tale for the doorman.

I don't think Jack had an answering machine. If he did, I never saw him use it. He simply picked up his phone when it rang. He didn't even have a separate business line. I suppose that made sense because just about everybody who called him was considered a friend.

Jack didn't go out much. He didn't hang around the clubs. I remember his going clubbing with us only once. It was a humid summer night and we made stops at the Gate and the Vanguard down in the Village. I could tell he wasn't comfortable with a lot of insincere schmoozing.

I don't think he ever took even a long weekend off, let alone a vacation. He called our place in Northfield "the country." He had a standing invitation to visit but never did. I expect he had hosts of similar offers from friends around the world. But at the end of the day, he was content to pour a glass of scotch and put up his feet right there in his second-floor corner apartment at 39th and Park.

The line between work and leisure was so blurred with Jack I don't think even he knew where one stopped and the other began. Perhaps it was so overlapping there was no line at all.

Jack never went to church, never discussed religion. Yet he was one of the most religious persons I've ever known. He practiced what others only preached. His reputation with musicians, club owners, and promoters was the same – an ethical man who treated you with respect.

The kitchenette in his apartment was small even by New York standards. I don't think he minded. He didn't spend much time there. Once a week, an eager young man from Gristede's market delivered a small loaf of Pepperidge Farm white bread, thinly sliced ham, a few Red Delicious apples, and ginger ale. With less regularity he brought coffee, milk, mustard, and other provisions.

During the Christmas season, irresistible sweets were added to Jack's cupboard – homemade cookies of all kinds – 13 varieties of chocolate chip cookies; sugar cookies in all shapes and sizes; Mexican wedding cookies; peanut butter cookies with surprise twists; oatmeal cookies with spices; all baked with love in our sunny yellow-tiled kitchen. When we had exhausted our funds, energy, and creativity, Takashi would pack the cooled cookies in plastic bags with red ribbons.

Finally he would make a batch of his chocolate fudge, just in case Jack tired of cookies and got hungry for candy.

We'd go to Atlantic City and board the #319 bus for the 2½ hour ride up the Parkway to Port Authority and then trek across 42nd Street and down to 39th and Park, where we'd give a big bag of treats to whichever doorman was on duty.

Then it was up the elevator to Jack's place, where Sally Batson or one of a succession of secretaries would welcome us. When Jack got off the phone, where he seemed to spend most of his time, he'd come and greet us with open arms. Year after year, he would feign surprise at the multiple bags of sweets and thank us profusely. We would have a soda and chat between his phone conferences.

We always left with the great feeling that comes from spreading the true Christmas spirit and doing a mitzvah for someone you love. We had made Christmas cookies for a wise man.

Our final holiday season with Jack was in December, 1981, when he was 66 and still in remarkably good health, no high blood pressure, no heart problems, nothing to worry about.

Then in early November 1982, we got a call from the office that Jack had fallen in the bathtub due to a brain aneurysm. He had been taken to St. Vincent's Hospital where he lay in a coma. He died there on January 19, 1983.

Everybody, including his physician, was puzzled. How could this happen with no warning signs? Finally the doctor asked Jack's daughter, Nancy Maccini, if anything traumatic had happened in her father's life recently, because in some cases aneurysms can be brought on by such an event. Nancy relayed the story of her mother's recent death from cancer in October, 1982.

They hadn't lived together in 20 years, but each declared the other was "the only one I ever loved." I would soon experience first-hand that sometimes the only way for love to survive is to let go of one another.

The Scoop on Making Really Good Cookies

Don't over beat them.

Beat eggs into the dough one at a time

Bake cookies on the center rack of the oven.

Ovens vary. Watch cookies closely. There's a short space of time between a perfect cookie and a burned one.

Unless otherwise directed in a recipe, remove baked cookies to a wire rack to cool before stacking them in a container. This will keep them from sticking together.

Cool the cookie sheet between batters.

Original Toll House Cookies
– 5 dozen cookies

These yummy cookies filled with chocolate chips were Takashi's favorite. Hopefully, they were Jack's favorite too, because he got a lot of them every year.

2¼ cups all-purpose flour
1 teaspoon baking soda
1 teaspoon salt
1 cup butter, softened
¾ cup white sugar
¾ cup firmly packed brown sugar
1 teaspoon vanilla extract
2 eggs
1 12 -ounce package Nestle' Toll House Semi-
    Sweet Chocolate Morsels
1 cup chopped nuts

Preheat oven to 375 degrees.

In a small bowl, combine flour, baking soda, and salt. Set aside. In a large bowl, combine butter, white sugar, brown sugar, and vanilla extract. Beat until creamy. Beat in eggs. Gradually add flour mixture. Stir in chocolate morsels and nuts. Drop by level measuring tablespoons onto ungreased cookie sheets. Bake 9 to 11 minutes. Let stand 2 minutes before removing to wire racks to cool.

Variations: Stir one of the following into the dough:

½ cup crushed candy canes

⅓ cup M&M candies

⅓ cup butterscotch flavored chips

⅓ cup peanut butter chips

½ cup raisins

½ cup shredded or flaked coconut

⅓ cup cut-up dates

⅓ cup almond brickle chips

1 tablespoon grated orange peel

½ cup caramel chips

COOK'S NOTES
IMPROVISATIONS
& VARIATIONS

Oatmeal Chocolate Chip Cookies
– 3½ dozen cookies

½ cup white sugar
¼ cup tightly packed brown sugar
¼ cup butter, softened
¼ cup shortening
1 egg
1 teaspoon vanilla
2 tablespoons milk
1 cup all-purpose flour
¾ teaspoon salt
½ teaspoon baking soda
1 cup quick-cooking rolled oats
1 6 -ounce package semi-sweet chocolate pieces
½ cup chopped walnuts

Preheat oven to 375 degrees.

In mixing bowl, cream together sugars, butter, shortening, egg, vanilla, milk. Combine flour, salt, baking soda, oats, chocolate, and walnuts. Stir into creamed mixture. Drop from a teaspoon 2 inches apart on greased cookie sheet. Bake 8 to 10 minutes. Let stand 1 minute before removing to wire rack to cool.

COOK'S NOTES IMPROVISATIONS & VARIATIONS

Outrageous Oatmeal Nutmeg Cookies
– About 45 cookies

¾ cup Crisco shortening
1 cup brown sugar
½ cup white sugar
1 large egg
¼ cup water
1 teaspoon vanilla extract
1 cup all-purpose flour
1 teaspoon salt
½ teaspoon nutmeg
½ teaspoon baking soda
3 cups uncooked rolled oats

Preheat oven to 350 degrees.

Place Crisco in a large bowl. At high speed, beat in brown sugar, then white sugar. Continue beating 1 minute. Beat in egg and water. Beat in vanilla extract. Reduce speed to low and gradually beat in flour after you have sifted it. Add salt, nutmeg, and baking soda. Use a large wooden spoon to stir in oats. Drop by regular teaspoons 2 inches apart on greased cookie sheet. Bake 12 minutes or until golden brown. Tops should be springy when lightly touched. Allow cookies to sit on cookie sheet 1 minute before removing them to a wire rack to cool. Store in an airtight container.

COOK'S NOTES IMPROVISATIONS & VARIATIONS

Cranberry Oatmeal Cookies
– 2 dozen cookies

^{2}/$_3$ cup butter, softened
^{2}/$_3$ cup brown sugar
2 eggs
1½ cups old-fashioned rolled oats
1½ cups flour
1 teaspoon baking soda
½ teaspoon salt
1 6 -ounce package dried cranberries
^{2}/$_3$ cup white or semi-sweet chocolate chips
  (optional)

Preheat oven to 375 degrees.

Using an electric mixer, beat butter, softened, and brown sugar together in a medium mixing bowl until light and fluffy. Add eggs, mix well. Combine oats, flour, baking soda, and salt in a separate mixing bowl. Add to butter mixture in several additions, mixing well after each addition. Stir in cranberries and white or chocolate chips.

Drop by rounded teaspoonfuls onto ungreased cookie sheet. Bake for 10 minutes or until golden brown. Leave on cookie sheet for 1 minute before removing to wire rack to cool.

COOK'S NOTES IMPROVISATIONS & VARIATIONS

Super Easy Peanut Butter Cookies
– Abut 24 small cookies

1 cup sugar
1 egg
1 cup crunchy or creamy peanut butter
1 teaspoon vanilla

Preheat oven to 350 degrees.

In medium bowl, beat sugar and egg until well mixed. Add peanut butter and vanilla. Mix well. Drop by teaspoon onto ungreased baking sheets. Press each with tines of fork. Bake about 9 to 11 minutes until cookies are light brown around the edges.

Let cookies sit on the baking sheets for 3 minutes before removing to rack to cool. Cookies will continue to bake during the 3 minutes.

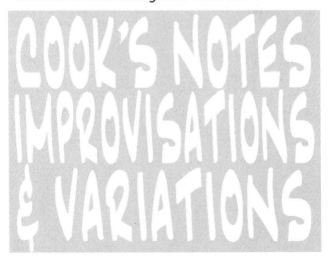

Playful Peanut Butter Cookies
– About 15 cookies

¼ cup shortening
¼ cup peanut butter
¼ cup brown sugar
1 egg, beaten
¾ cup sifted flour
¼ teaspoon baking powder
$1/8$ teaspoon baking soda
$1/8$ teaspoon salt

In a bowl, mix together shortening, peanut butter, sugar, and egg. Add flour, baking powder, baking soda, and salt. Chill in the refrigerator for about an hour.

Preheat oven to 375 degrees.

Take dough out and roll it into balls, each containing about a measuring tablespoon of dough. Place 3 inches apart on cookie sheet. Press down each ball with a fork. Bake 10 to 12 minutes. Let cookies stand 1 minute before removing them to wire rack to cool.

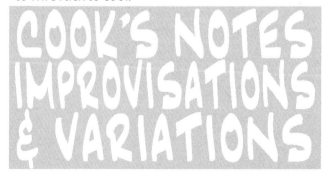

COOK'S NOTES IMPROVISATIONS & VARIATIONS

Peanut Cookies
– 5 to 6 dozen cookies

1 cup butter, softened
2 cups firmly packed brown sugar
2 eggs beaten
2 cups all-purpose flour
½ teaspoon salt
1 teaspoon baking powder
1 teaspoon baking soda
1 cup Wheaties cereal
2 cups quick-cooking rolled oats, uncooked
1 cup chopped salted peanuts

Preheat oven to 400 degrees.

In a large mixing bowl with an electric mixer, beat butter and brown sugar until fluffy. Blend in eggs. Sift together flour, salt, baking powder, and baking soda. Add sifted flour mixture to butter mixture; mix well. Stir in cereal and oats, then stir in peanuts.

Drop dough by teaspoonfuls onto lightly greased baking sheet. Press with a fork to flatten. Bake 10 to 12 minutes, or until done. Leave on baking sheet 1 minute before removing to wire rack to cool.

COOK'S NOTES
IMPROVISATIONS
& VARIATIONS

Mexican Wedding Cookies
– about 4 dozen cookies

½ pound butter, softened
½ cup confectioner's sugar plus more for
  dusting
1 teaspoon vanilla
¼ teaspoon salt
2 cups flour

Preheat oven to 375 degrees.

Cream butter with ½ cup confectioner's sugar, vanilla, and salt until fluffy. Stir in flour. Chill 30 minutes or until firm enough to handle.

Shape into 1-inch balls. Place balls 1 inch apart on ungreased cookie sheet and bake 12 to 15 minutes or until light golden. Leave on cookie sheet 30 seconds.

Remove to wire rack and dust heavily with sifted confectioners sugar. Allow cookies to cool on wire rack. Store in airtight container in cool, dry place. Just before serving, sift more sugar over cookies.

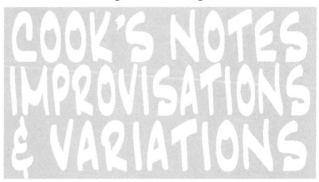

COOK'S NOTES IMPROVISATIONS & VARIATIONS

Fudge – *3 pounds*

3 cups sugar
¾ cup butter, softened
²/₃ cup evaporated milk
1 12 -ounce package semi-sweet chocolate
  pieces
1 7 -ounce jar marshmallow crème
1 teaspoon vanilla

*Combine sugar, butter, and milk in saucepan and
bring to rolling boil, stirring constantly. Continue
boiling over medium heat and stirring constantly 5
minutes. Remove from heat and stir in chocolate.
Add marshmallow crème and vanilla. Beat until
blended. Pour into greased 13 x 9 inch pan. Cool
at room temperature.*

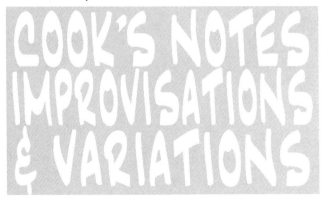

Photo by Jerry Stoll

Art and Dr. John,
two badass cats
sportin'
bigass hats.

Thanks to Casey
Stoll for giving
permission to use
the photo of Art.

Photo by Nunu

In a N'Awlinz Groove

The place a cat's born ain't necessarily the place he's from. He could be from anutha zone entirely. Bu was born up in Pittsburgh, but he was as filled with the spirit of New Orleans as he could be.

Dr. John

ATLANTIC CITY - It's Christmas night, 2009. The year is coming to an end, and my emotion driven bumpy journey writing this book is too.

I'm mellowed out, curled up on the sofa. WWOZ New Orleans is streaming in from the French Market on the computer. I turn it up a few notches. Nobody home next door to complain.

Next thing I know Snake is playin' my favorite version of Bobby Timmons' "Moanin', you know the one I mean, the original recording of this tune with Bobby on the piano. Life is sweet.

I call Snake to thank him. Turns out he moved down to New Orleans from Ventnor, New Jersey, the little town that borders Atlantic City on the south. We talk a while about Art, how he's been gone 19 years, his and my love affair with NOLA, and the book. I tell him I'll keep in touch.

If Dr. John were here tonight, he'd say I'm at the N'Awlinz Dis Dat or D'Udda part of the book. Yeah, he'd be right on the money.

Bob Dylan would know what he's talkin' about. Dylan devoted most of a chapter to New Orleans in *Chronicles Volume One.* He said, "There are lots of places I like but I like New Orleans better... The city is one very long poem... New Orleans, unlike a lot of those places you go back to and that don't have the magic anymore, still has got it... Around any corner, there's a promise of something daring and ideal and things are just getting going."

Art once put it like this: "Being in New Orleans is like having one foot in Europe without having to change your money. Damn! It's even better than Europe in the wee small hours. The music never stops, and there's always some place to get somethin' good to eat and a whiskey." His passport should have said he had dual citizenship – New Orleans and then the rest of the U.S.

So here's to you, N'Awlinz, you lovable ol' gaudy, bawdy, rough around the edges, warm 'n cuddly, swell hell of a place. I guess it was just natural that you and Art would have a big gushy, smoochy love affair 'cause drums are one humongous part of your roots. And did I mention that Art, too was a lovable, ol' gaudy, bawdy, rough around the edges, warm 'n cuddly, swell hell of a place?

Wynton Marsalis laid it all out when he said about Art:

He was the greatest man most of us will ever know... He was just made of something else, different from us mere mortals... He stayed on the road shaping excellent band after band, long after most of his generation and younger had faded and curled like bad, old and loud wall paper. He loved this music and the musicians that played it and they loved him back even under the most adverse circumstances (of which there were many).

He loved to swing and help others to swing. That's what he did full out, all night long – daytime too - all the time!... He was a great storyteller who loved and knew intimately all sorts of people from criminals to judges. Yes, and they loved him because he was a magician and everyone loves magic.

He was no saint, but a hero bred to battle. Possessed of an inborn fire that could not be doused. A hot, passionate combination of fury, calm, greed, generosity, intelligence, and soul, yes, that is what he was most of all – unconquerable.

(Foreword to *Art Blakey's Jazz Messages* by John Ramsay, Manhattan Music, Inc., 1994)

Teenage brothers Wynton and Branford Marsalis joined the 11-piece Jazz Messengers Big Band in 1980. The band with second drummer John Ramsay debuted at the Bottom Line in New York City June 19 after only three rehearsals.

Art and I stood in the back of the room watching and listening like a couple of new parents. I leaned over to Art and whispered, "They're all good but Wynton has that Lee Morgan stage presence, as if he was born to be right where he is. He's totally at home up there."

Art grinned, nodded his head, and made his way through the crowd to join the guys: Billy Pierce, tenor sax; Bobby Watson, alto sax; Branford Marsalis, baritone and alto sax; Valery Ponomarev, trumpet; Wynton Marsalis, trumpet; Robin Eubanks, trombone; Kevin Eubanks, guitar;

John Ramsay, drums; James Williams, piano; and Charles Fambrough, bass.

The School of Blakey had expanded and Professor Blakey himself was on top o' the world. A good thing, too, because there was no time for tinkering. In three days, they'd be headed to Europe for the jazz fest circuit including Kongsberg, Montreux, and Northsea.

Wynton, I know you're reading this so I gotta tell you my favorite memory of you on this whole tour. Between bus breakdowns on those treacherous, narrow mountainous Italian roads, you danced up and down the aisle of the bus with Pasha, our little curly black poodle in your arms.

Branford, don't think you're getting off easy. I've got a favorite memory of you, too. Remember that fabulous five course dinner the people in one of the Italian villages threw for the band? I think everybody in town came out for it. Anyway, Art and I were seated at a different table from the band. Takashi was hanging out with you and Bobby Watson. I know you'd already taken a lotta shit from the ten-year old who got away with far too much teasing of the band just because of who he was.

Well, I figure you got him back that night letting him drink all the wine he wanted, and he wanted a lot. The kid had the worst hangover of his life the next morning. It was sooo bad Guisippi refused to drive the bus anywhere but the nearest hospital until Art threatened him. After all, first things first. We had to get to the next gig.

As I'm finishing typing the Branford/Takashi saga, out of the blue, I'm reminded of something memorist D.G. Fulford once said: "Family histories are in plain sight… Take a look around… the hats… the belts… the shoes."

That takes me back to a park bench in Lexington, Kentucky, in June, 2009. I had just told Mac (Dr. John) the awesome news about having a Louisiana publisher for the book when New Orleans drummer Shannon Powell joined us. "Hell, yes, a book about Art belongs with a Louisiana publisher. Bu had more New Orleans spirit than a bunch of people who lived all their lives in the state. I'd see him every once in a while. He was a New Orleans foodie for sure. He loved Buster Holmes' red beans and rice. I remember like yesterday him coming out of Buster's place wearing his trademark western hat, boots, and one of those muscle shirts with the sleeves cut out."

I thought, Shannon, you're right. New Orleans is a hat town, and Art's were bigger and badder than most. You could say that about a whole lotta Art's parts.

Next time I saw Shannon was in November at a Wednesday night jam in Irvin Mayfield's Jazz Playhouse tucked away in the Royal Sonesta on Bourbon. Shannon got on the mike, introduced me, told the crowd about the book, and said they'd better buy it. His announcement was greeted with cheers, applause, and well wishes. Yeah, Shannon, right again about where this story should slide out of the womb.

Lying in bed that night, I was picturing that if Art were still alive, he'd be a fixture sitting in at the club whenever he was in town. He always loved everything about the Royal Sonesta, and the club would be just one more thing.

Then, if Mac was in town, there's a good chance he and Art would head for the kitchen to make drunken shrimp.

Dr. John's Shrimp New Orleans
aka Drunken Shrimp – *2 servings*

New Orleans is the best place for shrimp and music in the country!
Dr. John

1½ cups extra-virgin olive oil
¼ cup butter
1 clove garlic, halved, unpeeled
1 tablespoon Italian dry seasoning mix
1 bay leaf
1 teaspoon seasoned pepper
1 teaspoon cayenne pepper
1 pound (21-25 count per pound) Gulf shrimp
  with heads, unpeeled
¼ cup white wine
Salt to taste
1 loaf French bread, heated

Heat oil, butter, garlic, Italian seasoning, and bay leaf in large skillet. Sauté about 8 minutes until garlic is soft. Add seasoned pepper and cayenne pepper and cook 3 more minutes. Add shrimp and cook over low heat 5 minutes until shrimp turn dark pink. Add wine and salt. Pour shrimp and sauce into serving bowl and serve with the hot bread for dunking.

After they'd licked their shrimp bowls clean and finished off some of Mac's rabbit stew, they'd go out in their sartorially splendid virile headgear, which they hadn't bothered to remove while eating anyway, and take over a few clubs. No such thing in New Orleans as these bold badasses keeping a low profile even if they wanted to. Late night would turn into morning, and Art would start thinking about breakfast. As he said, "There's always some place to get somethin' good to eat and a whiskey."

Winding up the clock, I'm reminded of a recent conversation with Herman Ernest, III in the Green Room at the Highline Ballroom in NYC. If you've been to a Dr. John and the Lower 911 concert sometime in the last eon, you know Herman's the sheer talent and raw energy behind the drums. He's the guy who goes on the mike, gets you up off your ass, and keeps you dancing till you get funky butt. Did I mention he's from New Orleans?

When I told Herman I was almost finished with the Art memoir, he looked me in the eyes and said, "Bu ain't dead. He'll never die. He still swings with all of us through the musicians who came through Camp Blakey. The music they continue to make and pass on is the living Art Blakey... He influenced young musicians in and out of his bands. You didn't have to be in the Messengers to be touched by him. And it wasn't just the things he taught them technically. He taught them by example to have fun with the music. Nobody was better at that than Bu."

"He was a hell of a guy off stage, too. But I won't go there. Those stories are x-rated. That's all I'm gonna say about that."

O.K., back to the food. I'm including all three of our banana pudding recipes along with the catfish po' boy and muffuletta. When I'm anywhere near Bourbon Street, I still get my daily muffuletta, sweet potato chips, and banana pudding at my favorite neighborhood deli, the Quartermaster, where they can do no wrong 24/7.

Old-Fashioned Scratch Recipe
Banana Pudding – *4 servings*

½ cup sugar
2 tablespoons flour
¼ teaspoon salt
2 cups milk
3 eggs, separated
¼ cup sugar
1 teaspoon vanilla extract
50 vanilla wafers
4 medium ripe bananas, sliced

Preheat oven to 425 degrees.

Mix ½ cup sugar, flour, and salt in saucepan. Slowly add milk, stirring until everything is smooth. Heat to a full boil over medium high heat, stirring almost constantly. Reduce heat to low and continue to cook for 15 minutes, stirring occasionally.

Beat egg yolks in bowl. Add just a little of the milk mixture to the yolks and stir. Add yolks to the milk mixture gradually. Cook on low for 5 minutes. Remove from heat and add vanilla.

Line bottom of 1 quart casserole dish with 25 wafers. Top with 2 sliced bananas. Cover with 1 cup of the custard mix. Repeat layers ending with custard.

Beat egg whites until stiff. Slowly add ¼ cup sugar and continue beating until stiff peaks form. Spread over pudding. Bake at 425 degrees for 5 minutes or until barely browned. Serve warm or chilled.

COOK'S NOTES IMPROVISATIONS & VARIATIONS

Southern Shortcut Banana Pudding
– 4 servings

1 3¼-ounce package vanilla pudding
2 egg yolks, slightly beaten
2½ cups milk
25 vanilla wafers
2 large bananas, thinly sliced

Non-dairy whipped topping, whipped cream or meringue, optional but highly recommended. Check out recipe for meringue under Old-Fashioned Scratch Recipe Banana Pudding.

Combine pudding mix, egg yolks, and milk in saucepan. Cook and stir over medium heat until mixture comes to a full boil. Remove from heat.

Put vanilla wafers on bottom and sides of 1½ quart baking dish. Add a layer of banana slices and pudding. Continue layering wafers, bananas, and pudding, ending with pudding. Eat it as is or top it.

Banana Boat Pudding
– 4 servings

1 3¼ -ounce package vanilla pudding
1 cup non-dairy whipped topping
1½ cups miniature marshmallows
Vanilla wafers
2 bananas, thinly sliced

Prepare pudding according to package directions. When the pudding is chilled, fold in the whipped topping and marshmallows. Line a glass pan or casserole dish with wafers. Pour in half of the pudding. Cover with the bananas. Add the rest of the pudding. Chill.

Pan Fried Catfish Po' Boys – *4 servings*

The Fish:

4 catfish fillets
Freshly ground black pepper to taste
Yellow cornmeal
3 tablespoons, more or less, extra-virgin olive oil

Rinse fillets and wipe with paper towel. Heat the oil over medium heat in a large skillet. Dip fillets in cornmeal.

Fry the fish until browned on one side, about 3 minutes. Turn and fry until done, about another 3 minutes. Blot with a paper towel.

The Bread:

French bread rules.

The Dressing:

Shredded lettuce, thinly sliced tomatoes, sweet onions, pickles, and mayonnaise of your choice. Kick it up a notch with Creole mayonnaise, homemade tartar sauce, or remoulade sauce. You can quickly whip up the tartar sauce by adding drained pickle relish, in an amount of your choice, to mayonnaise.

Accompaniments: A bottle of Louisiana Hot Sauce and a plate of lemon wedges.

COOK'S NOTES IMPROVISATIONS & VARIATIONS

Muffuletta – *2 really big or 4 regular servings*

The olive salad: This is my version of a recipe
I saw on the back of a postcard in a Bourbon
Street shop.

¾ cup green olives, finely chopped

¾ cup black olives, finely chopped

3 more or less, cloves garlic, minced

1 anchovy fillet, mashed, optional but highly
recommended

1 tablespoon capers

¼ cup parsley, finely chopped

½ cup, or an amount to your taste, extra-virgin
olive oil

Freshly ground black pepper to taste

*Mix everything, cover it, and refrigerate until you're
ready to use it. This tastes even better after a night
in the fridge.*

The other stuff:

1 round of sourdough or Italian bread

½ pound hard salami, thinly sliced

½ pound prosciutto or ham of your choice,
thinly sliced

½ pound provolone cheese, thinly sliced

Assembly:

*Slice the bread down the middle horizontally.
Scoop out about an inch of bread from both slices.
Slather both slices with liquid from the salad. If
you like extra oil, add it now.*

Layer salami, prosciutto, and provolone on the

bottom half. Top it generously with olive salad. Eat it now or put it in a big plastic bag and refrigerate it until you're hungry. Take it out of the fridge about 15 minutes before serving. Cut into portions.

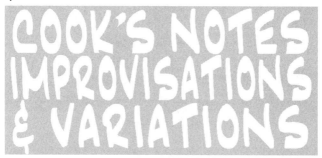

COOK'S NOTES IMPROVISATIONS & VARIATIONS

I want to shout out to my mandolin playing Daddy's spirit before I close this N'Awlinz chapter. His favorite singer was Fats Domino and his all-time favorite song was "Walkin' to New Orleans." He was always talking about taking me to a Fats concert, but we never got there.

Anyway, Daddy, I want you to know I'm writing my way back to New Orleans. The road is wide and friends are by my side. I'm gonna let Bobby Charles know how much you loved "Walkin'". Daddy, he's the guy who wrote it for Fats. Damn, maybe Bobby, Mac, and I can even stick a pole in the water and tell each other some really outrageous fish tales. Hallelujah!

Atlantic City – 5:25 p.m. New Year's Eve, 2009. Dave, down at WWOZ, cued up "Blues March" from the *Moanin'* album, and I'm dancing around the room. Another year almost finished. Another chapter completed. Gotta put on my red suede boots and party tonight.

Addendum: The irreplaceable Bobby Charles died the morning of January 14, 2010 while this book was still in progress.

Bobby, God bless your beautiful soul. I will play and replay your new CD, *Timeless*, the tribute to Fats, when it comes out on my birthday, February 23. There's so much more I want to say to you and about you, but you were such a private person, I won't put anymore in print. I'll find another way to let your spirit know what's in my heart and mind. Meantime, this chapter is dedicated to you.

Photo by Cezanne Wish Nails @ Dockside Studio

Two true friends, Bobby Charles and Mac Rebennack (Dr. John), at Dockside Studio where they recorded Timeless, Bobby's last CD before he died. Thank you Cezanne, for this magnificent remembrance of Bobby.

© Ebet Roberts

Art groovin' on his final CD with Dr. John
and "Fathead" Newman.

Unraveling and Remembering

All changes, even the most longed for, have their melancholy, for what we leave behind is part of ourselves.

Anatole France

It was already oppressively hot when the Allied moving van pulled up to the side of the house at 8 a.m. that Friday morning in August 1983. Art escorted the two friendly but business-like young men through the house, our home, pointing out which items were to be loaded on the truck and taken to an empty Bleeker Street apartment in Greenwich Village. This new place wouldn't be our home; it would be Art's alone. He said he wanted Takashi and me to be there often. How nice it would be to have a place in the City, he reminded me. A place where we could hang out and stay over when we come in for all the things we love about New York: museums, restaurants, shopping, jazz clubs, etc. I found comfort in his words, whether they would come true or not. Even though I had told Art I could no longer share a bed, a home with him, I couldn't imagine our lives not touching. After all that had happened, we still shared a soul and the care and nurturing of a beautiful child. Up to now, Art had been my home, my caregiver, my life. Alone, I wasn't sure who I would be.

I heard him telling the movers, Jim and Thomas, that yes, the black baby grand piano would go, as would the blonde wooden and glass handcrafted case that had housed his exquisite porcelain doll collection. The dolls already had been carefully boxed. Movers were not to touch anything else in the garden-like living room of floral sofas and white wicker.

Only one thing was to be removed from the den: the deep brown velvet sofa bed. Nothing would be disturbed in the dining room and kitchen.

Upstairs they would take only Art's oak roll-top desk and trunks of custom tailored shirts and other clothes. The house would not look empty. I was grateful for that. Art asked if I'd be all right with Takashi accompanying him to the City and staying for the weekend. Knowing it would make the transition easier for both of them, I said "Fine." I gave each a silent bear hug, certain that if I said even a word, I would burst into tears.

I went back inside and did what I always do when I need to think things through. I brewed a pot of green tea and sat at the oval oak kitchen table Art had had hand-crafted by a Greenwich Village artisan.

My thoughts wandered back to that August night in 1968 when we met at Slug's and had no expectations of one another except for him making music and me enjoying it.

I surveyed our years together and tried to pinpoint where life had gotten so far off the track that I could no longer live with this man who had been everything to me. Hadn't I known there would be other women in his bed when he was on the road for weeks and months at a time? Hadn't I known he wasn't comfortable alone and always needed someone for company? Hadn't I known jazz groupies hit on musicians every night? Wasn't I secure in the fact that no matter whom he flirted with at the club or whose bed he shared after the gig, it didn't diminish his love for me and our life together? Love, after all, was not a rationed commodity. It was immeasurable.

So what was the turning point that brought us to this final separation? I realized it was his openness. That sounds strange doesn't it? Counselors tell us openness is desirable in a relationship. For me it was callous and poisonous. I got sick at my stomach every time I heard him on the phone making arrangements for his current roadie or Jack to get plane tickets for the woman who would accompany him on his next gig. He freely gave out our unlisted phone number to women who would call expecting me to take messages regarding their upcoming rendezvous with him. While I was away, one even slept in my bed and left her lipstick-stained glass on the bedside table for me to see.

When confronted, Art's answer was always the same: "You know I'd never leave you for any of them. I love you."

I was dying, and our relationship was dying right in his arms, and he thought telling me he loved me would fix it. I vacillated between overlapping depression, drinking, and fits of anger. One minute I'd be lying in a fetal position, sobbing. The next I'd be slamming the back door so hard it broke, and going room to room throwing things. I shattered picture frames and tore up photos of Art and of us together. I shredded his address book and broke his glasses. At the end of the day, wine and vodka only added to the pain.

I don't know exactly when or how I rid myself of the destructive behavior, but eventually I did. I also convinced Art that I was serious about separating, and he, with Jack's help, found the Bleeker Street apartment. In a short while, I'd have to give up the house and most of its contents. I couldn't even afford to have the block long yard mowed.

Takashi and I wept, packed, and wept some more. Neither of us knew who we'd be when we closed the back door and headed for a nondescript apartment several miles away. The house on Mill Road had been such a part of us that leaving was an act of spiritual and mental mutilation.

A loneliness and void deeper than I could ever have imagined took over my days and nights after the separation. It started right there at the kitchen table on Art's moving day. I can't say precisely when it began to lift, but I can tell you writing was my salvation. It eased the wounds and loneliness in a way nobody or nothing else could. I wrote to and about Art in a stack of journals. Private entries he would never see. Words about two loving people in better times. The journals are gone. I don't know where. What I have written below reflects my memories of some of those entries and more. Recollections of days and nights filled with love and wonder and then, in the end, death.

And in the sweetness of memory let there be laughter, and the sharing of pleasures. For in the dew of little things the heart finds its morning and is refreshed.

Kahlil Gibran

So, dear Art, here are some recollections that warm

my soul with humor, tenderness, validation...

My favorite part of nights at home was getting my hair brushed. You sat on that big overstuffed chair in the bedroom and I on the footstool. You held each section of hair in your left hand and gently brushed it with your right. I was in ecstasy. No wonder I kept my hair long all those many years.

When I said I wished I'd met Picasso, you sent me off to Paris to meet his paintings. Later, his exhibit came to the Museum of Modern Art and you waited patiently in a line stretching down the block with me on that stormy Sunday for three hours.

I should have known when I was reading a stack of sociology books by Harvard professors that you'd give me a scholarship to that very university to learn from them first-hand in summer symposiums.

Then there was the time I mentioned my desire to study yoga again. Not finding it practical to go off to India at that very moment, I convinced you I could learn just as much from Yogi Shanti Desai right over the bridge in Ocean City.

And there's the story of Bookends, our bookless book-store. A thousand yellow business cards with brown print clearly listed us as the proprietors. Problem was our shelves were bare. You'd played the concert at Stockton College, gotten paid, and cashed the check. The money to stock the store was in your back pocket. All that was left to do was to bring home the cash and call the book distribu-tor to schedule delivery. You almost made it. You got as far as American Appliance, only a short distance from our house, before you stopped to go shopping. When all was concluded, we got next-day delivery on a matching washer and dryer, a dehumidifier for the basement, and a carload of things listed as small audio equipment. We would never want for portable radios or tape players again in life. You were so proud that we could bypass the laundromat and wash and dry clothes at our leisure in our newly dehumidified basement. You neglected to mention we'd also have to bypass Bookends. For what it's worth, I still have a Bookends souvenir business card. Don't know what happened to the other 999.

Speaking of shopping, you're the only person I ever knew who actually enjoyed taking coupons and grocery list in hand and spending the afternoon at the supermarket. Of course, I didn't really expect you, the improviser, to follow the list. We had some exotic meals with the food you came lugging home, didn't we?

When you were away, I treasured all your notes and letters. Sometimes I could decipher your large, bold script, and other times I gave up. Whether I could read it or not, the message of caring was there. And when I put my nose to the page, I could smell you.

Your mark on me is permanent. As Faulkner said, "The past is never dead. It's not even past."

After you left, I felt lost and adrift in the brass king-size bed and resorted to sleeping on the floor in that old green sleeping bag. I washed the towels over and over but the bathroom still smelled of your Aphrodesia cologne. I stop and stare when I pass another man wearing that scent.

In the twenty years since you went into the studio for the last time and recorded *Bluesiana Triangle* on March 5, 1990, until right now, I've never been able to talk to anybody about it, not even Tim or Mac, and you know I can spill out just about anything to them. It's still all bloody raw emotion for me. Damn, I'm getting a lump in my throat already.

I know we always felt like we could read each other's minds and finish each other's sentences. But, at the end, when you were so weak and could barely talk, I didn't understand what you were trying to tell me when you kept saying, "Play the record. It's for you, Egghead. Play the record." You'd squeeze my hand and your voice would trail off.

Hell, I didn't even know what record you were talking about. Maybe we'd been apart too many nights and mornings before you asked me to your bedside at the end. Maybe I'd lost the ability to read your mind.

Finally, sometime after your death, somebody, I don't remember who, gave me a tape of *Bluesiana Triangle*. (See note on p.182.) Sometimes I'd turn the volume up full blast and realize you were telling me the big stuff in the way you knew best. Other times, I'd get the cassette out, open it, and put it back out of sight unplayed. I couldn't listen to you, picture you painfully growing sicker with cancer before it cruelly silenced you altogether.

Here's what I came to understand over time and tears. When you called Mac to set up the recording session, you knew you were dying. You didn't tell him or "Fathead" or anybody else because you wanted the focus to be on music and message not sickness. You wanted to play a farewell love letter to New Orleans, and who better to collaborate on that than Mac? A no brainer. You also wanted one more chance to give back to the planet and you three agreed a percent of the profits would go to the National Coalition for the Homeless. You had always given quietly without fanfare to people and causes that needed help. I still respect your wish for anonymity on a lot of the good you did.

I realized why you said, "This record's for you." You figured I needed to know you were ready to get on outta here and didn't want a lotta sloppy tears or heroic measures blocking the exit. You figured I'd get a smile out of your doin' Cuz's "Life's a One Way Ticket" with that last line you'd made famous through the years: "I ain't seen an armored car at a funeral yet," or as you usually put it to newbie band members and audiences alike, "You never see an armored car following a hearse."

That song definitely let me know "Don't expect any inheritance, baby. We spent it all on one hell of a ride, and I ain't accumulated any money since we split."

And just in case I didn't get the message first time around that you were ready to check out, you repeated it in "Next Time You See Me" and "When the Saints Go Marchin' In."

All along, you knew Mac and I were destined to become soul mated friends. You just didn't think it would take me so long to go introduce myself to him and find that out for myself.

"Need to Be Loved," the shake-your-ass instrumental written on the fly by you, Mac, and "Fathead", needed no interpretation or explanation. You knew you'd be loved as long as there was breath in my body and then a little longer.

When it came to "For All We Know," I think you pictured me smiling at your going full circle back to the piano where it all started. You'd been secretly waiting for that opportunity for a long time. And there you were singing, too. Damn, you must have thought I was a broken record all those years telling you to put that powerful, gritty voice on record. Now you did, only it wasn't big and gritty. It was little and weak. But the words were sweet and strong as New Orleans coffee, and I wrapped my arms, my head, and my soul all around them. You know I could recite the lyrics to every tune you ever dedicated to me and that's a hell of a lot of words.

For All We Know

For all we know we may never meet again

Before we go make this moment sweet again

(You sang the second line as "For all we know

this may only be the end.")....

Words by Sam M. Lewis, music by J. Fred Coots.

Sing your death song and die like a hero going home.

Shawnee proverb

Charcoal and pencil drawing by Jeff Schwachter, 2010

Art Blakey remembered with love and respect.

A Certified Death

You never really lose anybody you have
loved… What you have become because
of loving them is how they will be with you
always… Love is eternal.

Daphne Rose Kingma, Author

I'm holding and staring at Manhattan Certificate of Death 156-990 057702. It lists the name of the deceased as Art Blakey and date and hour of death as October 16, 1990, 1:45 p.m.

A doctor at St. Vincent's Hospital, whose name I can't read, certifies that traumatic injury or poisoning did not play any part in causing death and that death did not occur in any unusual manner and was entirely by natural causes.

This orange-and-white piece of paper bearing the Department of Health's raised seal goes on to say the decedent's usual occupation – the kind of work done during most of his life – was musician, and the other name by which the decedent was known is Abdullah Ibn Buhaina. He was born in Pittsburgh October 11, 1919. Line 18 says he was fathered by Bertram Blakey, but line 19 for maiden name of mother is blank.

"The decedent's corpse will be transported from the John H. Joyce Funeral Home, Inc. to Trinity Crematory October 21."

What this one-page Bureau of Vital Records document can't impart is on that October afternoon, our planet lost an incredibly gifted drummer who had led the Jazz Messengers since 1955. I lost the most influential person ever to touch my life – companion, sage, confidant, parent, child, and lover. He had been all that and more at one time or another during the last 22 years.

At the end, the tiny, cancer ravaged soul I cradled in my arms bore little resemblance to the larger-than-life man I had met at Slug's light-years earlier.

His last words, in that familiar gravely voice, were "I always loved you."

Musicians at Jersey Shore Jazz
Vespers honor the memory of
the proud drummer who once
was their neighbor.
Photos courtesy of Sandy Warren

Note for page 175:

Bluesiana Triangle musicians are: Dr. John - piano, Hammond organ, guitar and vocals; Art Blakey - drums and vocals (piano on "For All We Know"); David "Fathead" Newman - saxophones and flute (backup vocals on "Shoo Fly"); Essiet Okon Essiet - bass (backup vocals on "Shoo Fly"); John Bosadio - percussion (drums on "For All We Know").

List of Recipes

The Blakey smile and spirit live on in our grandchildren, Layla and Kaden.

Photos courtesy of Beth Blakey

Award winning music and food writer, Sandy Warren, and drummer Art Blakey shared a lot - loud laughs, salty tears, soft king beds, lumpy twin beds, one burner hot plates, big-ass gas ranges, tender words, cruel acts....Sandy stirs it up and shares it with the rest of us in *Art Blakey Cookin' and Jammin'*.

While you're digesting this, she's probably in Atlantic City walking the beach or curled up on her sofa. Either way, you can bet she's got a pad and pen in her hand.